critical acclaim

Rev. Sekou is one of the most courageous and prophetic voices of our time. His allegiance to the legacy of Martin Luther King, Jr. is strong and his witness is real. Don't miss this book! **-Cornel West, Professor of Religion, Princeton University**

The essays in *Gods, Gays, and Guns* are the result of deep immersion, in suffering and struggle, yes, but also in the ideas, political, theological, artistic, and above all democratic, that may make a difference. Sekou offers no simple answers. Instead, he gives us something rarer and more valuable: a book of powerful questions. **-Jeff Sharlet, Author, New York Times bestseller *The Family***

This is a hopeful book. The "occupy" movement has stirred awareness here in America and elsewhere that we may be on the threshold of momentous change. But where will the fresh ideas, the leadership and, most importantly, the sustaining spirit for such a change originate? Rev. Sekou's energetic, thoughtful and engaging book begins to answer some of these questions, and indeed the author himself embodies some of those answers. **-Harvey Cox, Hollis Professor of Divinity, Harvard University**

Provocative essays pertinent to today's headlines, written in the prophetic tradition by an ardent young preacher who lives and thinks in the vibrant space between Martin Luther King and Tupac. Reverend Sekou will shake up your thinking and settle down your spirit in the true manner of an inspired pastor willing to acknowledge his own religious doubts on the way to calming yours." **-Benjamin Barber, Author, *Jihad vs. McWorld***

Rev. Sekou's book offers a compelling critique of the problematic modalities of religion and democracy in the neoliberal and imperial U.S. His captivating essays in *Gods, Gays, and Guns* convinces me that Osagyefo Sekou's vision and voice are integral to the struggle for a genuinely just and participatory democracy. -**Faye V. Harrison, Professor of Anthropology, University of Florida**

Rev. Sekou has given us a book of passion, brilliance, and inspiration, *Gods, Gays, and Guns* lives and breathes with the Bible and its insistence on justice and compassion. - **Susannah Heschel, Eli Black Professor of Jewish Studies, Dartmouth College**

Gods, Gays, and Guns is a powerful and provocative manifesto that challenges old perceptions about race, sexuality, gender and power. Its theoretical brilliance is complemented by the author's accessible literary style and eloquence in the theological arguments advanced in this critical study. Rev. Osagyefo Uhuru Sekou has produced a monumental treatise that offers hope and courage, not only for the oppressed, but all humanity. **–Manning Marable, Author, *Malcolm X: A Life of Reinvention***

Rev. Sekou reveals himself as truly a pastor to the whole world. As a good shepherd, he is always to be found wherever his flock is most hurting, where its cries most express the underlying horrors we all would rather not name or notice. But he does, in Haiti, on Wall Street, among London's impoverished suburbs, in his own life. *Gods, Gays, and Guns* is what the gospel of the twenty-first century looks like—globalized, radicalized, and often seemingly heretical. **–Nathan Schneider, Senior Editor, *Killingthebuddha.com***

Other works by Osagyefo Uhuru Sekou

Book

urbansouls (2001)

Film

Exiles in the Promised Land:

The Quest for Home (2009)

Gods, Gays, & Guns

essays on religion

and

the future of democracy

rev. osagyefo uhuru sekou

campbell & cannon press

cambridge, ma/london, uk

Campbell & Cannon Press
955 Massachusetts Avenue, #175
Cambridge, MA 02139

Earlier versions of some of the chapters appeared in the following publications: "From New Orleans: A Prayer for Maids and Maintenance Men," *Louisiana Weekly*, October 2006; "Gods: Toward a Contemporary Discourse on Religion and Democracy", *Journal of Ecumenical Studies*, vol. 42, no. 1 (Winter, 2007);

"What Meaneth Black Suffering?: Race, Meaning-Making, and Democracy in Post-Katrina America", *The Fellowship Magazine*, Fall 2007; "The god of my Grandparents", *Brooklyn Rail* (January/February 2008); "Vocation of Agony: A Personal Reflection on Dr. King's Legacy", *The Fellowship Magazine*' Spring 2008; "Who's god?: Faith, Democracy, and the making of an authentic Religious Left", *Dispatches from the Religious Left: The Future of Faith and Politics in America* (lg: New York, 2008) ; "Gays are the New Niggers: A Tribute Bayard Rustin", www.killingthebuddha.com, June 2009; "The Last Nail", www.killingthebuddha.com, August 2009; "Dear God from Haiti", www.killingthebuddha.com March 2010; "Queering Democracy and Christianity", www.feminstwire.com , April 2011; "Cornel West and the Crisis in Black Leadership", www.feminstwire.com, May 2011; "A Prophet in Exile: A Personal Meditation on James Baldwin," www.thefeministwire.com, August 2001; "Hip Hop, Theology, and the Black Church", *The Black Church and Hip Hop Culture: Bridging the Generational Divide* (Scarecrow Press, 2011); "Catch A Fire" *Vibe Magazine*, December 2011/Jaunary 2012

ISBN-13: 978-0-615-58370-9

dedication

for francis kissling

contents

preface

Democracy and god have failed. While these essays are an acknowledgement of the divine and democratic failure, they are bound up in a hope that humans, if not a god, have the capacity to end empires and break into history a new meaning of humanity. This volume lays bare my crisis of faith. Beginning with personal narratives, my writing seeks out the various ways in which humans make meaning for themselves in light of circumstances not of their own choosing. I have been horrified at the rapid decay of opportunities for the historically othered at home and aboard yet heartened by their capacity to seize upon the best of themselves and bend history to their will.

Fellowships with Catholics for a Free Choice, Brooklyn Society of Ethical Culture, Judson Memorial Church, Institute for Policy Studies, Ohio State University's Kirwan Institute for the Study of Race and Ethnicity, and New York Theological Seminary's Micah Institute have provided space for public discourse, political action and written reflection. Democrats Aboard-Paris, France sponsored lectures related to this subject matter. A special note of thanks goes to a great assistant and a dear friend –CB Stewart.

I am indebted to Rosemary Ruether, Beverly Harris, Fred Clarkson, Nicole Spigner, Nathan Schneider, Robert Kenner, and Ethan Vessley-Flad for their critical editing and insightful comments. I have been informed by rich conversations with friends, colleagues, elders, and professors: Tamura Lomax, Or Rose, Michael Brandon McCormack, Kathy Engel, Constance Borde, Zachary Miller, Danny Glover, Javiela Evangelista, Belvie Rooks, Dedan Gill,

Walter Hidalgo, Michael Ellick, Drew Dellinger, Conrad Tillard, Melanie Harris, Congressman Dennis Kucinich, E. Stephan Epps, Ealy Mays, Anasa Troutman, Astra Taylor, Joe Strife, Mariama White- Hammond, Tannie Stovall, Jeff Mansfield, Jee Kim, Julie Johnson Staples, Hannah Hofheniz, Marisa Egerstorm, Jay Williams, Emira Woods, Andre Perry, Tricia Sheffield, Bill Dobbs, Jill Williams, Jake Lamar, Joia Crear-Perry, Fredrick Holmes, Shannon Flam, Jim Haynes, J. Evert Green, Taleigh Smith, Yunus Tuncel, Harvey Cox, Gary Dorrien, Diane L. Moore, James Cone, Donna Schaper, Warren Goldstein, Bishop John Selders, Judith LeBlanc, Councilwoman Attica Scott, Christopher Morse, James Lawson, James Forbes, Jee Kim, Lord Frank Judd, Marcus Raskin, Robin Templeton, James Early, Leslie Cagan, Daisy Machado, Vincent Harding, and Walter Wink. Cliff, Laura, Michelle, and Gloria—the generous staff at Andover-Harvard Theological Library—have been a source of encouragement as well as my adoring mother in law, Euda Facey and dotting Aunt Shirley.

Most of all, I am privileged to be partnered with "my companion at the gate"-- Karlene Griffiths Sekou.

Rev. Osagyefo Uhuru Sekou

Cambridge, MA

Perhaps the primary distinction of the artist is that he must actively cultivate that state which most men, necessarily, must avoid; the state of being alone. –James Baldwin

The artist must never side with the makers of history but rather those who have been the victims of it. –Albert Camus

vocation of agony

Sitting in our favorite coffeehouse, Tyler Jared, my eldest son, and I are having our "man time." I am sipping a cappuccino and he is drinking some orange concoction. We stare into one another's eyes, with an occasional "What?" breaking our silence. We are excited to see each other and saddened by the time we have spent apart. I hold a deep sense of calling that has taken me around the world, but away from him and his siblings. He has grown so much. He is now taller than me, his 13-year-old face starting to break out with pimples, voice cracking, but he is still my baby.

I hold his hand and run my fingers through his golden locks. It embarrasses him, but he does not stop me, because I am Dad. He interrupts the silence. "Dad, everyone knows you want to be like Martin Luther King." Blushing and flattered I respond with a flat attempt at humility. "No, no, son, I am just trying to stand in tradition that keeps track of human. . ."

Annoyed, Tyler cuts me off. "No, Dad, everyone knows." He raises an eyebrow. "You risk arrest," he states. (He is reminding me of the scolding he gave me for being arrested at the White House, when, much to his chagrin, his teenage cohorts could have seen me being handcuffed on television. I was not practicing what I preached, since I always told him to stay out of trouble, and then went and got myself arrested!)

"You organize other preachers. You talk about world peace." After a pregnant pause, he announces, "But you are not that good at it!" Before I can defend myself – and the entire project of freedom – he notes: "You know that they started another war in Lebanon. Did you know that?"

To my surprise, Tyler had been paying attention to world affairs, including Israel's bombing in Lebanon in the summer of 2005. He was clear that if I had been "good at it," there would not be yet another war in the Middle East. With the wisdom of a teenager, Tyler concludes, "Look, you should give speeches about it and write a book about it. But you are not that good at making it happen." And I am left speechless.

So then what does it mean to honor the legacy of Dr. King? Maybe, it means moving into projects of Chicago and living with gang members in their tenement slums, as he did in 1966. King lived on $6,000 a year with four children because he believed in serving the poor over personal gain. He took a $1 (one dollar!) annual salary from SCLC. It is often noted that he had three suits the last year of his life, and that he washed out his dress shirt in the sink at night to have it clean for his next day's speaking engagement.

King gave every dime he had to the Movement, including the $100,000-plus award that accompanied his Nobel Peace Prize. When rebuked by his own board at SCLC, he still spoke out against the Vietnam War, only to be further chastised by every major national newspaper. When trashed publicly by Malcolm X, Stokely Carmichael, Bull Connor, and southern city fathers, King never lashed out in anger but always responded as a loving statesman. With death threats abounding, the FBI discrediting his work through its COINTELPRO program, and SCLC funding in question, he went to march with sanitation workers in Memphis – broke, black garbage men.

Rabbi Heschel along with Rev. Dr. William Sloane Coffin, Rabbi Balfour Brickner, Rev. Dr. Walter Wink and others founded Clergy and Layman Concerned about Vietnam. It was before a gathering of this controversial audience at the historic Riverside Church that King delivered his troublesome speech, "A Time to Break the Silence" on April 4th, 1967. In that speech, King also challenged the monopoly on religious discourse shaped by conservative religious individuals and institutions:

> Some of us who have already begun to break the silence of the night have found that the calling to speak is often a vocation of agony, but we must speak. We must speak with all the humility that is appropriate for our limited vision, but we must speak.

That night, King issued to America yet another stirring warning, responding to her terrible engagement against the people of Vietnam:

> The war in Vietnam is but a symptom of a far deeper malady within the American spirit, and if we ignore this sobering reality we will find ourselves organizing clergy- and laymen-concerned committees for the next generation. … We will be marching for these and a dozen other names and attending rallies without end unless there is a significant and profound change in American life and policy.

At the Riverside Church in New York City on March 21, 2005 – the same venue where Dr. King had delivered his hallmark "A Time to Break the Silence" speech almost 40 years earlier – I became the founding national coordinator of Clergy and Laity Concerned about Iraq. That night, in a bright yellow blazer and shiny black pumps, Susannah Heschel preached heaven down.   Quietly she began to read the King James Version of Second Samuel the twelfth chapter, verses one through seven:

> 1And the LORD sent Nathan unto David. And he came unto him, and said unto him, There were two men in one city; the one rich, and the other poor.
>
> 2The rich man had exceeding many flocks and herds:
>
> 3But the poor man had nothing, save one little ewe lamb, which he had bought and nourished up: and it grew up together with him, and with his children; it did eat of his own meat, and drank of his own cup, and lay in his bosom, and was unto him as a daughter.
>
> 4And there came a traveler unto the rich man, and he spared to take of his own flock and of his own herd, to dress for the wayfaring man that was come unto him; but took the poor man's lamb, and dressed it for the man that was come to him.
>
> 5And David's anger was greatly kindled against the man; and he said to Nathan, As the LORD liveth, the man that hath done this thing shall surely die:
>
> 6And he shall restore the lamb fourfold, because he did this thing, and because he had no pity.
>
> 7And Nathan said to David, Thou art the man. . .

Sensing where she was going with the text, Rev. Dr. James Forbes, Senior Minister of the Riverside Church turns around to the clergy and politicians sitting in the pulpit and said: "Somebody, call the fire department, Susannah is about to set the place on fire." And she did. She used the story of David's murder of Bathsheba's husband--after an affair with Bathsheba, David coordinated her husband's death. Susannah compared the judgment of god delivered by the prophet Nathan to David to the judgment of god that she delivered to George Bush. In the tradition of talking back to the preacher, we stood up and shouted, "Go 'head and preach Heschel. "

She proclaimed: "George Bush, thou art the man, who launched a war on the people of Iraq based on a lie." "George Bush, thou art the man, who has attacked our civil liberties." After spewing a litany of sins committed against democracy by President Bush, She queried with fire, "George Bush, do you not know that the primary identity of god in the Old Testament is justice." The audience exploded and we were fulfilling King's prophecy because there had not been a "profound change in American life and policy." We used King's words as our liturgy, reading:

> We must rapidly begin the shift from a "thing-oriented" society to a "person-oriented" society. When machines and computers, profit motives and property rights are considered more important than people, the giant triplets of racism, materialism, and militarism are incapable of being conquered. . .

Rev. Jesse Jackson delivered a stirring sermon, where he posed the question, whose god is god? He described the way in which the religious right was using the name of god to justify the war on terror. Representing over 300 faith-based institutions working to end the war in Iraq, CALC-I filled a void of silence by religious leaders that had been evident in the first two years of the war. Less than six months after our founding, CALC-I and our parent organization, United for Peace and Justice, the nation's largest peace coalition, called for an anti-war march through the streets of D.C., lobbied Congress, and nonviolent civil disobedience at the White House.

As we planned for this three day series of events, we watched another tragedy unfold. A Category Five Hurricane descended upon the Gulf Coast and subsequently the levees around New Orleans broke. For five days American citizens were stranded on roof tops and in the Superdome. News media outlets referred to these black citizens as refugees. Given the multi trillion dollar drain on state and municipal resources, the troops and federal system was not prepared to handle such a catastrophe. Yet another reflection of King's prophesy, "Every bomb dropped in Vietnam explodes in Harlem". The bombs dropped in Baghdad now exploded in the lower ninth ward.

On September 26th, 2005 with the people of New Orleans in our hearts, we gathered about 15 blocks from the White House at Foundry United Methodist Church. A collage of Buddhist monks, Catholic priests, rabbis, theologians, agnostics, and atheists sang freedom songs and prayed for god to end the war in Iraq. We marched to the White House and asked for a meeting with President Bush. We were rebuffed. As planned, the group kneeled in front of the White House and prayed for the end to the war. It is illegal to pray in front of the White House. Over 370 people were arrested, including 60 clergy.

Yet, the war continued with the blessing of the religious right. In the face of world-wide opposition to the build up to the war and turning popular support of the war, the Bush administration continued to pillage the Iraqi nation, people, and oil resources with god on their side. Less than a year into Bush's second term and three months after the levees failed in New Orleans, I left the United States for the first time. In Paris, I explored the philosophy of liberation movements and reconsidered the prophetic tradition of the Black church.

Eventually, I returned to the United States with many more questions about god and democracy. New Orleans, which was a frequent topic of conversation in Paris, was in no better shape than when I left. The sustained suffering and governmental ineptness in New Orleans, only served to accelerate my crisis of faith. Seeking some answers, I moved to New Orleans to serve as founding Executive Director of the Interfaith Worker Justice Center of New Orleans.

After six months, hearing people call me "Reverend" often sent a chill up my spine, because most days I no longer believed in god. New Orleans had broken something in me. I could not get my head around religion, human suffering, and democracy. After accomplishing the less ambitious goals of developing the board of directors for the Interfaith Worker Justice Center, hiring staff, and opening a legal clinic for workers, I resigned and returned to New York and entered Union Theological Seminary.

Nestled between Columbia University's Teachers College, Jewish Theological Seminary, and Riverside Church, Union is the center for the study of liberal and liberation theology in the U.S. The self-contained campus-boasting the largest private park in Manhattan and the largest collection of religious books in the Western Hemisphere--was a welcomed respite. I needed time to pull back, think and maybe pray through the defeats that I suffered and my crisis of faith. I entered into Union with the haunting questions that disturbed me as the leader of CALC-I and the executive director of IWJ-NOLA. Reading and writing about progressive religion, liberation theology, and interfaith dialogue were illuminating.

Yet it was not enough. While the debates raged in classrooms, the quad, and bars, I was away from those who suffered the most on the ground. The isolation of the academy was indispensable yet insufficient. The time to think was essential. I realized that I wanted to move my primary site of struggle to the parish. There, in the needs of the people, their challenges and joys, perhaps then I would find an answer or at least a new set of questions about god and democracy.

Continuing to write on everything from gay marriage to Hip Hop, I returned to parish ministry. I served as the social justice minister at a Dutch reformed church in the East Village. I began to work with a group of homeless queer teenagers. A lot of these young people came from southern religious upbringings and were ousted out of their families for coming out. They caught the first thing smoking to New York where many of them lived on the street and were exploited in the sex trade. Our work was simply providing a hot meal on Sunday evenings and some skills training. As I came to know these young folks, I began to speak more forcibly about sexuality and gay marriage legislation that was pending and eventually passed in the New York State Assembly.

Many of them were just poor and broke, looking for decent and dignified work in a city that was experiencing the worst economic collapse in two generations. While our church was open and affirming to queer folks, their experience was one of vitriol and often exploitation at the hands of clergy. It became incandescently clear that I had to take up their cause in public space.

Shortly, thereafter, I was called to serve as the Senior Minister of Lemuel Haynes Congregational Church—a small, United Church of Christ congregation—located in South Jamaica, Queens, New York. The church, which is over 75 years old, is made of up of Black folks who came from the south and the Caribbean in search of a better life for themselves. They did not get rich in New York but they did okay. Most of my members achieved the America Dream --bought a house and put their kids through college.

Our congregation took up the work of a living wage campaign in New York City. Along side other churches, mosques, and synagogues, we embarked on a massive struggle to create a living wage standard in the nation's most wealthy city. The Fair Wages for New Yorkers Act was a small intervention in the market. It required developers who received over one million dollars in tax subsidies to pay a living wage as well as retailers who would occupy the new developments to pay the same. Clergy throughout New York and across denominations testified that our parishioners were struggling to make a dollar out of fifteen cents--a living wage is the just and moral thing to do. A cowardly City Council, in cahoots, with a billionaire mayor, powerful real estate lobby and spineless union, passed a toothless bill.

In the midst of my pastorate, the earth opened up and destroyed Haiti. Subsequently, I was part of a delegation that went and served in Petit Mon Village in Leogone, Haiti. Post-Katrina paled in the face of the tortured landscape of the first Black free republic in the Western Hemisphere. I was humbled in the presence of the Haitian people's resilience.

As I continued to move to sites of struggle through out the world, I experienced the spiritual fortitude of dispossessed communities. Two shots fired by Scotland Yard called me to Britain to cover the London riots and attend the funeral of Mark Duggan, whose police killing set the kingdom ablaze. I witnessed Duggan's family and mates of Broadwater Farm—a mostly Jamaican housing project in London—seek justice for their fallen son.

Eros and Sophia converged in such a way that I left the parish ministry, married, and re-focused on my studies. Love is a powerful force in the face of the most brutal empire in human history. It soothes and makes tender the rough places of our personality and predicament. Love means we care for the personal, political, social, economic, and organizational needs of others more than we do our own individual and organizational desires. Love is that force that cuts across human divisions of race, religion, nation, or creed. Again, King teaches us:

> When I speak of love I am not speaking of some sentimental and weak response. I am not speaking of that force which is just emotional bosh. I am speaking of that force which all of the great religions have seen as the supreme unifying principle of life. Love is somehow the key that unlocks the door which leads to ultimate reality.

Love sheds new light on the improvised language and build a new system of ideas and social infrastructure. As we love each other, we will create a loving society preoccupied with peace and justice. Conversely, our contemporary age has been shaped by anxiety-inducing events—ecological calamity, fiscal insecurity, and arbitrary terror. Ecological disaster strikes indiscriminately; the international fiscal crisis has engendered collective experience of economic demise; wars of revenge elevate the presence of death and despair in the day to day living of all who occupy the planet.

Geography, class, and pigmentation are no longer impenetrable shields. Even the citizens of the most powerful nation in human history live with a sense of vulnerability. These events, with all of their political effects and affects, suggest that what it means to be human is in flux-- the primary feature of the spirit of the age of angst—*zeitgeist der angst* . Our eschatological hope is to usher in the *zeitgeist der agape*—the spirit of the age of sacrificial love .

In order to accompany hope into history we must begin by telling the truth of the ugliness of the American empire—a vocation of agony. By highlighting the excesses of the empire and the vacuousness of the church, one is cast out of the traditional institutions and intuitions, but this is a gift. King used the hopes of an exiled people to transform American democracy. King's legacy is an outsider's legacy—which broke the back of American apartheid and unleashed a new set of democratic possibilities—precarious and fragile. Exile—the saddest fate as defined by Edward Said—offers an ever critical set of interpretations of the times in which we live. For that set of lenses I am grateful.

Having heard about the conversation between his elder brother and I , Gabriel Israel DuBois, my second oldest son, was not to be outdone. Known among his family members as the "sensitive one," Gabriel is the spitting image of me when I was seven. Getting eye to eye with me, he declares, "Dad, you know they shot Martin Luther King."

Bewildered, I can only say, "I know, son, I know."

"You know if you keep doing what you are doing they are going to shoot you, too … but I love you and will protect you…"

a prophet in exile

After the re-election of George W. Bush, I was done with America. Less than a year into Bush's second term, I left the United States for the first time. At the tender age of 34, I moved to Paris to be like James Baldwin. With money from a writing fellowship, I was confident that I was going to compose 'the book'; but I was not convinced that I would return to the States. In the City of Lights, I would walk, wander and wonder. Having been seduced not long before my move by French existentialism, I wrestled with what it meant to be a Black preacher with an artist's heart and a love for Sophia. I tramped about Paris, donning a black scarf, black sweater and black pants because that was Baldwin's attire when he first arrived in Paris.

I chose to live in Saint-Germain-des-Prés –the haunt of Albert Camus, Jean-Paul Sartre and Simone de Beauvoir. My small apartment was on rue Sabot and set above a café that was rumored to be where Baldwin and Camus had their infamous falling out. Every morning, I made my daily trek to the edge of Jardin du Luxemburg and into a cramped "bodega" owned by an Algerian family. After "salaam" and "bonjour," I went straight to the meat cooler, grabbed a block of cheese and baguette and swiftly made my way out the door. Frequently, I met other U.S. expatriate. Tanny Stovall—the Dean of Black Expats—held a weekly "Brothers" soirée in his flat near the Bastille. Having left the United States over four decades before, he knew just about every writer, painter, musician and intellectual who came searching in Paris. (I was just the latest casualty of American democracy.) Tanny told fabulous tales about "Jimmy."

Before day break one cold December morning, in a drunken stupor, I stumbled from the "Brothers" soirée to the train station, Gare de Lyon. With the aid of a faithful and meticulous translator and several cups of coffee, I was sober when I arrived to the Hotel de Ville de Lyon, where I was scheduled to deliver a lecture on humanity and nonviolence. In the well-appointed lecture hall, gold Baroque sculptures lit by fifteen wall-mounted chandeliers and an additional twenty or so hanging from the ceiling, I began my discourse with two quotes as existential bookends: "The artist must never side with those who are the makers of history but rather those who are the victim of it," admonished Albert Camus. In like manner, James Baldwin, my other soul mate, demanded that, "the artist must embrace that state of being that most men must necessarily avoid, that is the state of being alone."

After the lecture, I exchanged a few pleasantries with Mayor Gérard Collomb. He was a man after my own heart—a socialist and an admirer of Baldwin. And as most of my conversations with French intellectuals and politicians, he reminded me that I was "like" Baldwin, because I had come to France to write. There was a strange kind of freedom in Paris. It was the first time in my life that I did not experience the "burden" of race. In fact, my time in Paris was relatively privileged—my ideas mattered. Everywhere I went, soirées, cafes and bookstores, people wanted to know what I thought. Paris was the first place that I understood what it meant to be an organic public intellectual—using one's ideas to struggle for justice. After hours on end and several bottles of wine, I knew for what Baldwin was searching. I had found a space where I was free to think. Later, I would learn that this was not the case for Blacks born in Paris.

Le Devoir Collectif de la Mémoire, a mostly Arab and African group of Hip Hop artists, activists and at least one white Trotskyite, invited me to speak at their meeting. In November 2005, a young African man died as a result of being chased by the police. Hence, Arab and African youth, who already felt alienated from French society, expressed their rage by setting cars ablaze in Saint Denis and other Parisian suburbs. The Collective was responding to this crisis and asked me to give a talk on Hip Hop as an organizing tool. They encouraged me to attend a large conference that was being organized in Saint Denis at the University of Paris-VIII. Inevitably, they reminded me that Baldwin marched on their behalf in 1960s; and because I was "like" Baldwin, I must do the same. I attended the conference and marched in the streets chanting: *Fraternité! Liberté! Égalité!*

Living in Paris, provided me an opportunity to explore the philosophy of liberation movements and reconsider the prophetic tradition of the Black church. Reading and re-reading Sartre' *Existentialism as Humanism*, Camus' *The Rebel* and *The Myth of Sisyphus* and Baldwin's *The Fire Next Time*, the spirit of my grandmother was a constant presence. I missed the deep ocean of love in which the folks of the Arkansas Delta bathed me. Holding conversations in my head between Baldwin, Camus and my grandmother, I began to formulate a systematic consideration of existentialism, prophetic religion and activism. In James Baldwin, I was able to reconcile these traditions and would emerge from my exile with new philosophical lenses and theological considerations.

Millions of African-Americans migrated from the Jim Crow South in search of a better life. The North represented The Promised Land—free from the limits placed on Black mobility and opportunity that was so rampant in the southern states. In *Notes of a Native Son*, Baldwin recalls there was no milk and honey to be found:

> All of Harlem is pervaded by congestion, rather like the insistent, maddening, claustrophobic, pounding in the skull that comes from trying to breathe in a very small room with all the windows shut. . . Harlem wears to the causal observer a casual face; no one remarks that-considering the history of black men and women and the legends that have sprung up about them, to say nothing of the ever-present policemen, wary on the street corners-the face is, indeed, somewhat excessively casual and may not be as open or careless as it seems. If an outbreak of more of than the usual violence occurs, as in 1935 or in 1943, it is met with sorrow and surprise and rage...

In the face of such a violent existence, religion could offer a safe place. Though Baldwin left the church at the age of 17, the signs, symbols and songs never left him. Prophetic religion served to inform his project for years to come. Hence, the stories and songs of his childhood hold artistic and cultural significance. In *The Fire Next Time*, he recounts his conversation experience:

> I underwent, during the summer that I became fourteen, a prolonged religious crisis, I use the word "religious" in the common, and arbitrary, sense, meaning that I then discovered God, His saints, and angels, and His blazing Hell. And since I had been born in a Christian nation, I

accepted this Deity as the only one, I supposed him to exist only within the walls of a church-in fact, of our church-and I also supposed that God and safety were synonymous.

Upon graduating from high school he moved to Greenwich Village. Eventually, Baldwin felt that need that I know all too well: that he must leave the United States. Fifty-seven years before I began my exile, he set sail for Paris to be more than just a Negro writer. I followed him as he followed Richard Wright, and other artists—searching for freedom. The very place that he left to become a better writer was the very place to which he had to return, existentially, to finish his first novel.

The exilic Psalm 137 being played out on the Seine: Baldwin sat down at his river of Babylon, yea, he wept, when he remembered Harlem. In a 1961 interview with radio personality Studs Turkel, Baldwin recalled coming to honor his past:

> And I finally realized in Europe that one of the reasons that I couldn't finish this novel was because I was ashamed of where I had come from and where I had been, and ashamed of life in the church and ashamed of my father, ashamed of the blues and ashamed of jazz, and, of course, ashamed of watermelon, because it was, you know, all these stereotypes that the country inflicts on Negroes that, you know, that we all eat watermelon or we all do nothing but sing the blues, and all that. Well, I was afraid of all that, and I ran from it.

Using his religious epistemology, Baldwin made meaning out of the absurdity of being. Baldwin's fiction serves as an elegant and elongated description of the prophetic quest for meaning. His creative non-fiction served as terse prescriptive testaments. The title of his loving screenplay on Malcolm X, *One Day When I was Lost, was* gleaned from a popular African American hymn.

I know it was the blood

I know it was the blood

I know it was the blood for me

One day when I was Lost

He died upon the cross

I know it was the blood for me

The Evidence of Things Not Seen and *No Name in the Street* are both taken from scriptures that are prevalent in Black holiness discourse. Hebrews 11:1 reads "Now faith is the substance of things hoped for, *the evidence of things not seen.*[i]" *No Name in the Street* is taken from Job 18:17, "His remembrance shall perish from the earth, and he shall have no name in the street." *Go Tell it on the Mountain*, his semi-autobiographical novel, was drawn from the Christmas hymn announcing the birth of Jesus.

Go tell it on the mountain

Over the hills and everywhere

Go tell it on the mountain

That Jesus Christ is born

Go Tell it on the Mountain describes the life of the protagonist that is very similar to the life of Baldwin—a child preacher, in search of love from an unloving father, was not at home anywhere. James Baldwin was a prophet in exile. By prophet, I mean that his writing and activism called into question the prevailing norms, chastised the democracy and pointed us all to a new way of being.

Abraham Joshua Herschel notes in his book, *The Prophets*, that: "The prophet is human, yet employs notes one octave too high for our ears. He experiences moments that defy our understanding. He is neither 'a singing saint' nor 'a moralizing poet,' but an assaulter of the mind." Baldwin assaults the conventional wisdom of the day.

He sits in the pantheon of the existentialist prophets—Albert Camus, Jean-Paul Sartre and Simone de Beauvoir. James Baldwin embodied the existentialist quest for making meaning in a world that denied Black folks meaning. His being was in exile from Western democracy:

> I know in any case, that the most crucial time in my own development came when I was forced to recognize that I was a kind of bastard of the West. . . And this meant that in, some subtle way, in a really profound way, I brought to Shakespeare, Bach, Rembrandt, to the stones of Paris, to the cathedral at Chartres, and to the Empire State building, a special attitude.

My "special attitude" was prophetic existentialism—a religiously grounded critique of meaning and justice making in the midst of exile. Baldwin's writings are shaped by the constraints of racist and homophobic society and a freedom in exile. While homelessness and namelessness are features of exile, Baldwin turns them on their head to speak his special truth to the world.

A Prophet in Exile

When questioned by a report about being born poor, black and gay, Baldwin responded that he "hit the jackpot" because he had started so low in society. From the place of "lowness," Baldwin called upon our better angels by naming our demons.

In *No Name in the Street*, he critiques his childhood faith with democratic fire and prophetic brimstone:

> . . . in exactly the same way as the Christian church has betrayed and dishonored and blasphemed that Saviour in whose name they slaughtered millions and millions and millions of people. And if this objection might seem trivial, it can only be because of the total hardening of the heart and the coarsening of the conscience among those people who believed that their power has given them the exclusive right to history. If the Christians do not believe in their Savior (who has certainly, furthermore, failed to save them) why, then, wonder the unredeemed, should I abandon my gods for yours? For I KNOW my gods are real: they have enabled me to withstand you.

The Fire Next Time sustains Baldwin's indictment of America and extends to pathological self hate. In a letter to his namesake nephew, he cautions: "You can only be destroyed by believing that you really are what the white world calls a *nigger*. I tell you this because I love you, and please don't you forget it."

Baldwin unpacks what it means to be an exile without self love—a state which ate James Baldwin's father alive. Baldwin reflects on his step-father, the younger Baldwin's grandfather. "Well, he is dead, he never saw you, he had a terrible life; he was defeated long before he died because, at the bottom of his heart, he really believed what white people said about him."

Nobody Knows My Name confronts personal exile and its use in social critique. His early life was so tortured because of lack of love that he so desperately craved from his father. "Not merely the key to MY life, but to life itself." With his common agility, he leaps from the private to the public, personal to political, and landed firmly on the ground of being that is love-uncovering and the nakedness of the human experience:

> . . . when lovers quarrel, as indeed they inevitably do, it is not the degree of their pigmentation that they are quarreling about, nor can lovers, on any level whatever, use color as a weapon, This means that one must accept one's nakedness.

For Baldwin, the experience of love caused one to be free and bound; freedom as in the home of one's lover's arms and "a bondage which liberates you into something of the glory and suffering of the world." To love yourself is to live in exile, yet be free. Like the hymn undoubtedly sang in the church of his and my childhood, "When nothing else could help, love lifted me."

My Parisian sojourn concluded at the American University in Paris with a lecture entitled, Les émeutes et Espoir. I compared the plight of French Arabs and Africans to African American exiles, like Baldwin and myself. My grandmother's hope was at the heart of it all.

Shortly, thereafter, I returned to the United States. I, eventually, finished "the book." I have returned to Paris a half of a dozen times. Each time I am tempted to stay a little longer. The struggle for the least of these to which I was called continues to beckon me back the United States. I take solace in knowing that Baldwin marched with Martin Luther King, debated Malcolm X and shared the rally stage Bayard Rustin.

As a pastor I have used Baldwin's work and words many a Sunday. Still, every now and then, I get that nagging feeling that I should be, in Paris, writing. There is a simple truth about Paris, Baldwin and me. On rue Sabot in Saint-Germain-des-Prés, I did what Baldwin did –in my small flat I embraced the very thing I was running from.

whose god?

In the post-9-11 era, one has been able to interchange the words "Christian," "conservative," "religious," "right," and "Republican" in one sentence without necessarily changing the meaning of the sentence. A lexicon shift of this magnitude is an indication of profound meaning-making power.

The war in Iraq was and is often discussed by religious right as a war against Islam. Originally, then President George W. Bush named the misguided adventure as Operation Crusade, which harkened back to another holy war between Islam and Christianity. Between 1095 and 1291 the Crusades were a series of religiously-sanctioned military campaigns waged against mainly Muslims, by the Holy Roman Empire, with the aim to restore Christian control of the Holy Land. After some protest from the Saudi empire, the name of the Iraqi war was changed to Operation Iraqi Freedom.

The religious right blessed the imperial expansion by indicating that the war in Iraq was America calling by god to fight the evil Muslims in a post 9-11 world. Two days after 9/11, Rev. Jerry Falwell prophesied that god had lifted the hand of protection from the United States and allowed the terrorist attacks because "the pagans and the abortionists and the feminists and the gays and the lesbians."

Months after 9-11, he told *Time* magazine that "God" had chosen him to lead the world's war on terror. He confessed "God told me to strike at al-Qaeda and I struck them, and then he instructed me to strike at Saddam, which I did, and now I am determined to solve the problem in the Middle East."

From divining the war in Iraq to the late Jerry Farewell's proclamation that Katrina was god's wrath visited upon America for its tolerance of gays and other "deviant" behavior, this god had been strategically employed by the powerful to divide the electorate and impose restrictions on democratic opportunity. This god maintained a hegemony over our public discourse; a supreme being that was synonymous with empire and its economy—an imperial god. A god that launched a pre-emptive war and punished the most vulnerable was a god I wanted no part of. A religion that defended the powerful over the powerless was not my religion.

Hence, there must be many gods if not mini gods. I am attempting to name them in way that keeps track of the fallibility of gods constructed by humans, including my own. In this essay, using a lower case "g" is to lower our conception of gods so that no religion can claim to have sole access to the divine.

Consequently, god, is a poly-glyph- word that has multiple meanings at once. The word, god, is linguistic intervention that reflects a conservative ideology that historically limited democratic opportunity. I am arguing that the use of god talk in American public life is often a lot less about religion and more about public policy.

While some would suggest that religion breaks down into two distinct categories. I posit otherwise. The choice is not between fundamentalism and secularism; faith and reason; but rather a more sinister set of categories.

Whose god?

The history, culture, and constitution of the American democracy were born of a unique blend of Enlightenment sensibilities and religious strivings. The structure of American democracy was never based on religion versus science. For the founding of the nation there has been a delicate and contestant consideration of the role of religion inside democracy

To say the word god in American public discourse is to conjure up a number of images and ideas that serve to undermine democracy in name of religious freedom. What matters is whose god has access to political power will be the god that is the most powerful when it comes to making public policy. The American pantheon of religion then must be discerned in such as way that it highlights the best of the relationship between democracy and religion. I have come to believe that nothing less than an epistemic break on the magnitude of the founding of Christianity and the depth of the Protestant Reformation will save our democracy.

What has emerged over the last two decades is not a break, but a theological capitulation to the neo-liberal economy by religious and non-religious folks alike. For most, religion is a meaning-making activity. We humans use it to situate ourselves within a broader context in the face of dread, death, and despair because it offers us an eternal story when we are comforted with a finite reality. Given that the critical victory of the Right has been existential rather than political, any countervailing project must highlight the existential.

This intervention is critical to our understanding the way in which we derive meaning. To achieve such an aim, we must—as Cornel West often notes—take an on-tological risk that will lead to existential vertigo. What is at stake is how we make meaning for ourselves within the dual languages of religion and democracy. This must therefore be a central part of the task of re-visioning a Religious Left. And it will require great theological, spiritual, and political courage on our part.

Unfortunately, what has been taken by many to be an adequate popular countervailing religious argument is not up to the meaning-making task that is at hand. However, it does let us glimpse what we might call the neo-liberal god. By the neo-liberal god, I am referring to a religious movement in contemporary politics that has absorbed as its own the framework and policies of neo-liberalism.

In the same manner in which the religious right has sanctified the imperial aims of the Bush Administration, neo-liberal religious leaders have adopted the policy stances that bless neo-liberal political policies, which includes free trade, welfare reform, personal responsibility, and privatization of social services. These policies born out of the neo-liberal discourse provide the "talking points" for many religious leaders.

The most popular books written by an ostensibly liberal religious leader are *God's Politics* and *The Great Awakening*. Both books attack the supposed lack of religious sensibility on the political left and the religious right's monopoly on god-talk in the marketplace.

Both have reached the New York Times Bestseller list, and the books' author, Jim Wallis, speaks to sold-out audiences around the country. Despite his popularity,

Whose god?

Wallis and his Sojourners organization do not engage or take seriously the discourse of those it claims to serve—i.e. the poor—a discourse which is best embodied by the prophetic tradition of African-American religion.

Wallis' inability to claim the radical politics of the prophetic tradition serves to undermine the stated mission of his work, thereby limiting his capacity to articulate the development of an authentic Religious Left. Indeed, Wallis publicly argues against the organization of a Religious Left, arguing instead for a "moral center." While supporting a neo-liberal politic, Wallis often makes simplistic references to the prophetic tradition of the Black church—which reshaped the meaning of democracy by including those who had been historically "othered." Unfortunately, Wallis does not actually listen to this tradition.

Equally, his frequent claim that the Religious Right is dead is not only incorrect—it is dangerous. The Religious Right has defined two of the most fundamental activities of meaning making in human ecology-religion and politics. They have set the terms of the discourse in which all political discourse currently responds. We are unable to experience a radical break from this frame because the neo-liberal project merely changes the words, not the language.

While *God's Politics* devotes a lot of space to teaching the Democratic Party how to be better at courting religious voters, placing religion in the service of a political party is inappropriate, if not idolatrous. Wallis is concerned with developing new religious forces and claiming the mantle of promoting social justice. But how can he do this while largely ignoring one of the richest histories of social justice in the history of our nation—the prophetic black church?

I would go so far as to say that his misguided, unfair and divisive critique of the left serves not the poor and the greater good, but instead unintentionally enables the right and its efforts to roll back the gains of the Civil Rights Movement and a century of social progress. Despite this, Wallis has rightly identified that the younger generation hungers for social justice and spirituality. And, the success of his books may be fairly attributed to a widespread hunger for an alternative vision of religion and its role in politics.

This is the point at which I think we engage the possibility of a shift of such magnitude that an authentic Religious Left may find its heart, its head, its spirit and its voice. This is where I believe we have to go deeper, in order to set aside these essentially neo-liberal tracts that smooth over the rough edges, but don't fundamentally challenge the neo-liberal god; the god whose blue light flickers in the windows of the American night. And this is where we have to take a profound ontological risk, and confront our spiritual hunger, a hunger which requires us to reject the neo-liberal god.

The hope for an authentic Religious Left that can salvage our democracy lies in the genius and remarkable theological sophistication of African-American slaves. I believe their wisdom can serve as a guiding light to see us through the contemporary debates about religion and democracy. To begin among the poor and forgotten is both prophetic and revolutionary.

Whose god?

This essay is born out of my efforts to emerge from a personal crisis of faith. I found my own way out via the community which birthed me. There I found what I pray others will find as well—the course for the healing of democracy. History bears witness that the prophetic African American religious tradition that led me out of my despair also offers hope and possibility for the nation. We stand in the river of a great tradition whose flow can carry us to greater outpourings of social justice.

This essay makes two essentialist claims. First, that the black theological project is left-of-center. It begins, historically, with the humanity of black people inside the American empire, and the worship of the prophetic god, which is a left of center claim. Secondly, that the African-American religious tradition has always read the biblical narrative in close proximity to the sacred text of civic religion in the United States—the Constitution and Declaration of Independence.

These two streams that flow through our history and inform our contemporary discourse pose two fundamental questions: How have those who have been denied meaning made meaning of god and democracy? And, what can they teach us about our contemporary crisis? My answers to these questions necessarily begins with my story, and how I joined in the prophetic tradition of the African American church.

If Jesus is the author of my faith, then my grandparents were the editors. In rural Arkansas, I was raised in the ways of a Victorian, southern black woman who loved Jesus and justice. My grandmother, a proud Baptist, rescued me as a six-month-old from a fate that may have been too terrible to tell. A King James Bible and encyclopedias were my first gifts of memory. Later, my grandmother's admonishments, shaped by her god, posited existential gems that pointed to the measure of one's humanity: "You must never look down on people."

My grandfather, Reverend James Thomas, was a railroad worker and retired Pentecostal pastor. He possessed a third-grade education and yet was also possessed by a thirst for knowledge. He especially delighted in tidbits of black history that he had gleaned from folklore. The Bible was the book that he sought to master, and his greatest desire for me was that I also master that text in the struggle for justice. My grandfather may have only had a third grade education, but he articulated a vision of the world that was profound.

The most magical memory I have of my granddaddy "rightly dividing the word" was on a Friday evening, after the only factory in our town was threatening to close. With the community's economic vitality in question, granddaddy, black and burly, broad-nosed and big-lipped, stood at the sacred desk, looking out upon the sea of black and nearly broken faces. He "took" a text, as the congregation stood, the custom during the reading of scripture. Slowly and deliberately, he solicited, "If you will turn with me in your "Biiible..."—stretch ing the word to stress its significance—"to the gospel of John, the eleventh chapter and the thirty-fifth verse. When you find it, why don't you say, 'Amen.'"

"Amen," they responded, with great anticipation on their lips and even greater trepidation in their hearts. My granddaddy then whispered, in a tear-soaked voice, "And it simply, reads 'Jesus wept.'" Then, in the presence of a voiceless people, he made the book "talk," retelling the familiar story of Lazarus, where Jesus pleaded with his god to raise Lazarus so that others might believe. For over an hour, my granddaddy reminded a people that had been historically alienated, and were now demoralized and insecure, that they were the ones whom Jesus loved. Seamlessly blending Jesus' people's plight with the African-American struggle for freedom, my granddaddy's love for his people and the Bible merged in a way that was life affirming, and which rendered a hopeless town hopeful.

The signs, symbols, songs, and stories bequeathed to me in rural Arkansas resonated with powerful notions of justice for the poor, democracy for all, and god's desire for human freedom. Folks who were just two-and-a-half generations from slavery and functionally illiterate taught me the profundity of democracy and religion.

Among them was Mrs. Roberta. On documents that required her signature, Mrs. Roberta made her mark—an X—because she could not write her name. "Come here and read to me, boy," she would command with her hands on her walking cane and royalty in her voice. "Come here, boy, and read to me about our people." I obliged, with reverence.

In the singing, prayers, testimony, and other liturgical expressions of my youthful worshipping community, Jesus was hope in hopeless circumstances. Set against the darkness, Jesus and his god were the light. In the midst of what W.E.B DuBois termed the "frenzy," they shouted Jesus is "a bright and morning star," "water in dry places," "the lily of the valley," "the rose of Sharon," "a friend to the friendless," "a rock in a weary land," "a lawyer in the court," "a doctor in the sickroom," and a whole host of phrases that formed the essence of their belief in and about the divine and their situation, which began with an assumption of their worth and redemption. They knew that the darkness would not have the last word because god was with them. My grandfather's hopes, my grandmother's vision, and Mrs. Roberta's desires all flowed from a peculiar conception of god and democracy.

Called upon during the terrible night of slavery, the prophetic god told them to "tell ol' Pharaoh to let my people go." Their unsupervised and at times contested gatherings were a counter-hegemonic practice in and of itself. A people who had been historically denied access to the broader democratic project, and ultimately their humanity, affirmed their beauty, intelligence, and capacity while praying and working out their spiritual salvation and social freedom:

> We used to slip off in the de woods in de old slave days on Sunday evening way down in de swamps to sing and pray to our own liking. We prayed for dis day of freedom. We come from four and five miles away to pray together to God dat if we don't live to see it, do please let our chillum live to see a better day and be free, so dat dey can give honest and fair service to de Lord and all mankind everywhere.

The slaves did not leave a dense theological treatise to articulate their notions of power and freedom, because it was a criminal act for slaves to learn how to read. Thus, the permissible activity of singing was their first theological text. Ex-slave Vinnie Brunson recalled, "Dey sing 'bout de joys in de nex' world an de trouble in dis. Dey first jes sung de 'ligious songs, den dey commenced to sing 'bout de life here an w'en dey sang of bof ' dey called dem de 'Spirituals.'"

Reflecting death, misery, suffering, judgment, sadness, and hope, the spirituals served to articulate their situation and offer a sense of hope beyond their tragic circumstances. Oft times, the spirituals had dual meanings:

Swing Low, Sweet Chariot,

Coming fo' to carry me home.

Swing Low, Sweet Chariot,

Coming fo' to carry me home.

Well, I looked over Jordan and what did I see,

Coming fo' to carry me home?

A band of angels coming after me,

Coming fo' to carry me home

Lyrically, this song is a telling of the story of the prophetic god's entering into human history to take a faithful servant to paradise for reward, and an eschatological hope beyond the misery of the plantation. However, it was also sung as a signal that the Underground Railroad was near and that those who desired the reward of freedom on this side of the Jordan should get on board. And unlike the slave master's imperial god, their god deemed them worthy. With this in mind, a number of African-American religious individuals, institutions, and organizations worked to end the vicious system of slavery and expand democratic opportunity for themselves and their fellow citizens. A former slave named Isabelle Baumfree believed that that god changed her name to Sojourner Truth so that she could go about preaching the good news of freedom:

> My name was Isabella; but when I left the house of bondage, I left everything behind. I wa'n't goin' to keep nothin' of Egypt on me, an' so I went to the Lord an' asked him to give me a new name. And the Lord gave me Sojourner, because I was a travel up an' down the land, showin' the people their sins, an' bein' a sign unto them. Afterward I told the lord I wanted another name, 'cause everybody else had two names; and the Lord gave me Truth, because I was to declare the truth to the people.

Read in proximity of sacred documents of American civic religion, namely the Declaration of Independence and the Constitution, Sojourner Truth also breathed theological life into America's primary founding documents, the Declaration of Independence and the Constitution:

> Children, I talks to God and Gods talks to me. I goes out and talks to God in de fields and de woods. [The weevil had destroyed thousands of acres of wheat in the West that year.] Dis morning I was walking out, and I got over de fence. I saw de wheat a holding up its head, looking very big. I goes up and take holt ob it. You b'lieve it, dere was no wheat dare? I says 'God . . . , what is de matter wid dis wheat? and he says to me, "Sojourner, dere is a little weasel in it." Now I hears talkin' about de Constitution and de rights of man. I comes up and I takes hold of dis Constitution. It looks mighty big, and I feels for my rights, but der aint any dare. Den I says, God what ails dis Constitution? He says to me, "Sojourner, dere is a little weasel in it.

Whose god?

Harriet Tubman, the most successful conductor of the Underground Railroad, was called the Black Moses. She called upon her god to provide her with the strength to carry out the divine task of liberating others from the horrors of slavery:

> I had crossed the line. I was free, but there was no one to welcome me to the land of freedom. I was a stranger in a strange land; and my home, after all, was down in Mary land; because my father, my mother, my brothers, and sisters, and friends were there. But I was free, and they should be free. I would make a home in the North and bring them here, God helping me. Oh, how I prayed then," she said; "I said to the Lord, 'I'm going to hold steady on to you, and I know you'll see me through.

Tubman awoke one morning in 1862 singing, "My people are free! My people are free!" Later, reflecting on her nineteen dead-of winter journeys to liberate slaves, she wrote: "I just asked Jesus to take care of me, and He never let me get frost-bitten one bit."

In the twentieth century, progressive social movements called upon god to improve the conditions of the American working class. At the Progressive Political Convention of 1912, the delegates marched down the convention floor singing, "Onward Christian Soldiers." The Reverend George Washington Woodbey, pastor of Mount Zion Baptist Church, ran for Vice President with Socialist arty presidential candidate Eugene Debs. In a powerful dialogue with his Christian mother, Woodbey said he believed that god and the mission of Jesus were compatible with socialism. Eventually, his mother converted to socialism, but never surrendered Jesus. For

Woodbey, socialism—the democratization of capital—was the closest political system to the gospel.

The Civil Rights Movement was the last serious invocation of the prophetic god on American soil, as hymns and spirituals became songs of freedom. "I woke up this morning with my mind stayed on Jesus" became "I woke up this morning with my mind stayed on freedom." To the civil rights marchers, Jesus meant both existential and political freedom. "Somewhere we must come to see that human progress never rolls in on the wheels of inevitability," the Reverend Dr. Martin Luther King, Jr. proclaimed in one of his final sermons. "It comes through the tireless efforts and the persistent work of dedicated individuals who are willing to be co-workers with God."

The goal of his organization, the Southern Christian Leadership Conference was "to redeem the soul of the nation." King brought into the public space the prophetic African American evangelistic idiom in order to extend the rights of democratic citizenship to his people: "We have waited for more than 340 years for our constitutional and God-given rights," he proclaimed in his famous "Letter from Birmingham Jail."

"We will win our freedom because the sacred heritage of our nation and the eternal will of God are embodied in our echoing demands." The relationship between prophetic faith and the covenants of democracy shine most compellingly in his conclusion:

> One day the South will know that when these disinherited children of God sat down at lunch counters, they were in reality standing up for what is best in the American dream and for the most sacred values in our Judeo-Christian

heritage, thereby bringing our nation back to those great wells of democracy which were dug deep by the founding fathers in their formulation of the Constitution and the Declaration of Independence.

In what is considered his most "dangerous" speech, "A Time to Break the Silence," King invoked the spirit of Harriet Tubman and Sojourner Truth, declaring that the challenge of calling upon god in the struggle for social justice was a "vocation of agony." Indeed, he gave the speech in the midst of death threats, repudiation from the SCLC's board of directors, and merciless attacks in the mainstream and African-American media.

King invoked the prophetic god in denouncing "the giant triplets of racism, materialism, and militarism" and criticized the role of the United States in both the manipulation of foreign governments and its treatment of the poor (at home and abroad), which has led to the crisis of democracy we are experiencing today:

> A true revolution of values will soon cause us to question the fairness and justice of many of our past and present policies. On the one hand we are called to play the Good Samaritan on life's roadside, but that will be only an initial act. One day we must come to see that the whole Jericho Road must be transformed so that men and women will not be constantly beaten and robbed as they make their journey on life's highway. True compassion is more than flinging a coin to a beggar; it is not haphazard and superficial. It comes to see that an edifice which produces beggars needs restructuring.

This courageous oration transcended the details and consequences of the policies of the U.S. government in order to address the nature of religion and democracy, to show how they are in constant dialogue, and to reveal to us the religious precedents for democratic expansion.

In his last sermon, at Mason Temple Church of God in Christ in Memphis, Tennessee, King linked religion, democracy, and social protest, and demonstrated how they figured into an intimate conversation with striking Memphis sanitation workers:

> We have an injunction and we're going into court tomorrow morning to fight this illegal, unconstitutional injunction. All we say to America is, "Be true to what you said on paper." If I lived in China or even Russia, or any totalitarian country, maybe I could understand the denial of certain basic First Amendment privileges, because they hadn't committed themselves to that over there. But somewhere I read of the freedom of assembly. Somewhere I read of the freedom of speech. Somewhere I read of the freedom of the press. Somewhere I read that the greatness of America is the right to protest for right.

King then rhetorically addressed the question of the role of clergy in democracy, which was as tricky a question then as it is now: "Who is it that is supposed to articulate the longings and aspirations of the people more than the preacher?" He acknowledged the presence of clergy from around the country and challenged them to engage in what he called "relevant ministry":

> It's all right to talk about "long white robes over yonder," in all of its symbolism. But ultimately people want some suits and dresses and shoes to wear down here. It's all right tom talk about "streets flowing with milk and honey," but God has commanded us to be concerned about the slums down here, and his children who can't eat three square meals a day. It's all right to talk about the new Jerusalem, but one

day, God's preachers must talk about the new New York, the new Atlanta, the new Philadelphia, the new Los Angeles, the new Memphis, Tennessee.

Martin Luther King's understanding of religion and democracy cut hard against the dominant theology of his time, even within the African American church. In 1961, he and 2,000 other Baptist ministers were expelled from the National Baptist Convention because of King's and the other ministers' commitment to civil rights. Moreover, of the nearly 500 black churches in Birmingham, Alabama in 1963, less than a dozen participated in the Civil Rights Movement. The "Letter from Birmingham Jail" was partly written in response to local clergymen who found King's presence to be "untimely."

There will be analogous situations today for all of us who enter the prophetic tradition, as there have always been religious forces that have promoted or opposed democratic expansion. The Bible was used to justify slavery and segregation, but those who participated in the Underground Railroad had a different reading of scripture. Other times, it has been used to justify the status quo, or to do nothing in the face of oppression.

We can see this in the experience of the women's movement, and any other movement for democratic expansion. We certainly see it in the contemporary struggle over marriage equality. The reproductive rights movement traces part of its lineage to a group of United Methodist women meeting in a church basement in Dallas, Texas. What has moved history and expanded democracy has been prophetic minorities willing to risk life and limb to seize the public's imagination and transform politics and public policy. The thirteenth, fourteenth and fifteenth Amendments to the Constitution, the Civil Rights Act and Voting Rights Act are testament to this tradition.

I believe that an authentic and politically dynamic Religious Left can learn how the reading of scripture in close proximity to the sacred texts of American history and government can offer us a narrative of religious and civic discourse that is centered on the expansion of democratic opportunity. This has long been central to the struggles of African Americans, and is widely accessible and resonant in our culture in the stories of Sojourner Truth, Harriet Tubman, and Martin Luther King.

The Rev. Dr. Martin Luther King, Jr., "languaged" the prophetic god into public space. goal of his Southern Christian Leadership Conference was "to redeem the soul of the nation." The soul of a nation is its social structures, political discourse, and quality of life. Using evangelistic idiom to win democratic rights for African-Americans was a grand example of god-talk and democratic expansion.

I believe such a narrative can energize and inform a revival of the best of the prophetic tradition and provide a clean break from neo-liberalism and all its variants. This narrative is so powerful, so integral to our nation's history and our highest aspirations as a society, and has played such a profound role in the boldest, most successful movements for social justice, that it can salvage our democracy with an authenticity worthy of the founding of Christianity, and on a scale that could exceed the Protestant reformation. I realize that this vision will unbelievable to many. But just over hundred and fifty

Whose god?

years ago, it would have been inconceivable for me to be writing these words as a free man in my native Arkansas.

spiritual not religious

One hot June afternoon on the eve of Tupac Shakur's birthday, we gathered in the fellowship hall of Mt. Zion Baptist Church in Newark, New Jersey. The hall was suited for about 200 people but well over 500 people crammed in the space. Cameras and reporters swarmed and hovered as Hip Hop and young movement celebrities give selective interviews and posed for photojournalists and daunting fans alike. Reporters seemed stunned at the fact the words of "Hip Hop" and "politics" were being used in the same sentence. The occasion was the National Hip Hop Political Convention (NHHPC).

In the midst of a pivotal Presidential election of 2004, over three days, 6,000 or more youth activists, organizers, Hip Hop authors and journalists, and a few clergy gathered to contemplate the role of Hip Hop in American politics. The opening event of the convention at Mt. Zion Baptist sought to bridge the infamous generation gap.

With the war in Iraq, expanding prison industrial complex, crumbling public schools, and palpable breach between the Civil Rights and the Hip Hop generations, an intergenerational dialogue kicked off three days of intense debate concerning the political future of our generation and ultimately our democracy. Moderated by a youth pastor and movement elder, the dialogue included movement veteran Dr. Ron Daniel, Rev. Dr. Michael Eric Dyson, and I. I began my talk with a harsh criticism of the very institution that was hosting us and that gave me my voice-the black church.

I laid bare the level of mistrust engendered by some black church leadership and lamented the fact that number churches in our community are led by commuter shepards—self-serving pastors who drive luxury automobiles from well manicured suburbs to improvised inner cities to Sunday service. More often than not, the commuting clergy preached to a commuter flock--black middle class members of these houses of worship, who do the same as their pastor.

I noted that a number of young people in Hip Hop generation have been burned by the church. They have been exposed to a number of religious traditions, particularly Islam, and found at least a truth that helped them make sense of the world in their own image. Hence, I stated: "This is why a number of people in our generation say I am not religious. I am. . ." And on cue, over 500 young people bemoaned: "spiritual".

Nearly, four years later with another major presidential election pending, I recalled this experience at another historic gathering at Harvard Divinity School. This gather was sponsored by Harambee-the divinity's school black student organization. The symposium was entitled, "Hip Hop and its Religious sensibilities", yet, another pairing that puzzled reporters and Ivy League professors alike. This panel was a collection of theologians, clergy, a female Muslim divinity student, a Christian rapper, two African-American studies professors, a youth practitioner, and myself. As I re-told the Newark story to the Harvard audience, they on cue responded with the generational mantra: "I am spiritual."

Spiritual not Religious

In my first book, *urbansouls*, I meditated upon my experiences as a youth advocate and youth minister. As a result of the book, which this essay builds upon, I have been referred to as a "Hip Hop" theologian. Equally, I am a child of the black church- an ordained elder in the Church of God in Christ. I love the church. It saved my life and offered me the space to explore my gifts and celebrated me in the public presentation of those gifts. Yet this is not the experience of many of my peers.

These aforementioned experiences offer damnable critique of the black church and its relationship to Hip Hop and young people. Whether the setting is an inner city middle school, gang funeral, the nation's most famous school of religion, or a gathering of young political activists, the criticism of the black church remains unified. In their minds and lives, the black church is irrelevant to their life chances.

Moreover, there are not many theologians or scholars of religion who are attempting to craft a systematic theology or spirituality that takes youth voices seriously. This is in part due both the lack of value attributed to poor black and brown youth voices in the academy, the inability of the black church to relate to youth, and above all the sheer lack of courage among African-American religious leaders and otherwise to sit at the feet of young folks and engage them in sustained way. This lack of engagement is fueled a belief among older African-Americans and younger black folks with petite bourgeois sensibilities concerning youth. In word, the problem with black folks is young black folks -ala Bill Cosby.

As theologian and clergyman, three perennial questions haunt my existence: How do we end human misery? In light of said misery, how do humans make meaning for themselves in circumstances not of their own choosing? And what does our contemporary situatedness (circumstances) have to teach us about meaning making? Given that religion is primarily a meaning-making activity. Humans use it to situate themselves within a broader context in the face dread, death, and despair. Religion offers an eternal story in the face of a finite reality.

The foreboding gap between the black church and youth has lead youth to seek and create alternative spaces of meaning making. Hip Hop's saliency proves a space of meaning. Hip Hop reflects the situation of youth and their relationship to the church and society. Hip Hop reflects the situation of youth in America. And if the black church is to remain relevant in the 21st century is must ponder its relationship to Hip Hop, youth activism, and young people.

Treating young people as theological agents is sure to cause the same consternation that puzzled the reporters at the NHHPC and professors at Harvard Divinity. Hip Hop and theology are not typically shared in the same discourse. They are often seen as oppositional. In the preface to his book, *The Parallax View* philosopher and cultural critic Slavoj Zizek provides a metaphor for blending of seemingly unrelated topics:

Spiritual not Religious

A short circuit occurs when there is a faulty connection in the network-faulty, of course, from the stand point of the network's smooth functioning. Is not the shock of short-circuiting, therefore, one of the best metaphors for a critical reading? Is not one of the most effective critical procedures to cross the wires that don't usually touch: to take a major classic (text, author, notion), and read it in a short-circuiting way through the lens of a "minor" author, text, conceptual apparatus ("minor" should be understood here in Deleuze's sense" not "of lesser quality," but marginalized, disavowed by the hegemonic ideology, or dealing with a "lower", less dignified topic)? If the minor reference is well chosen, such a procedure can lead to insights which completely shatter and undermine our common perceptions.

By suggesting that young people are theological agents, both the historical theological canon and the sub-hegemony of the black church on religious discourse are short circuited. Given Hip Hop's impact on the life chances of youth, I want to position Hip Hop artists as para-theologians. The term para-theologian is inspired by St. Clair Drake insightful category, para-intellectuals. Hip Hop artist are persons outside the church and seminary are active consumers of theological knowledge and used that knowledge for intellectual, activist, and artistic purposes.

Secondly, I want to posit Hip Hop in part as a theology of existence- a systematic theology of ongoing critique of existence that is realized in everyday interactions and practices. Their theology of existence is partially shaped by the constraints of oppressive society and the hope experienced in said situation, therefore, honors their spiritual insights and proclivities by highlighting the theological and religious moments of Hip Hop music. The intent is not to develop a theological read of Hip Hop culture as means to help us see young people as theological agents, religious being, and spiritual creatures. Hence I want to challenge a new generation of scholars to take up three sentiments: 1) young people are theological agents; 2) Hip Hop houses a subterranean spirituality; and 3) the Hip Hop generation's critique of the church should not be valorized. It is more than valid is necessary for the redemption of the black church.

These considerations allow the possibility of a serious and rigorous engagement with Hip Hop as the potential euphemism of an emergent religion in late modernity. It pushes me to reconsider my role as pastor and theologian and may help us all be able to say with a straight face- I am a preacher.

dear god, from haiti

Dear god,

I have not written you in some time. I have been busy cleaning up your shit down here. I believe the last time I wrote you it was from New Orleans. Now, I write from a little further south—Haiti.

Our eleven person, multi-racial delegation was invited to Mon P'tit Village in Leogane, Haiti, which is about 25 miles outside of Port-au-Prince, near the epicenter of the earthquake. We are an eclectic embodiment of hope. An odd, at times combustible mixture—humanist clergy, dancer, theatre producer, horticulturist, professional volunteer, a loving do-gooder couple, and a Pentecostal bluesman—are the guests of two Haitian-Americans, Yoleine and James. They are educators in New York. Yoleine, a compassionate and gentle soul, is a guidance counselor; she has adopted a number of children in Haiti. James, a stern commanding figure despite flashes of glee and joy, is a high school principal. A decade or so before the quake that cracked the core of globalization, they founded the Neges Foundation, with ties to the Nobel Peace Prize laureate Wagria Mathia's green movement in Kenya. Mortgaging their comfortable positions to invest in the future of the wretched of the earth, they acquired land, then built and opened a green-education school in Leogane proper.

All commercial flights into Port-au-Prince were canceled. We had to fly in to Santo Domingo in the Dominican Republic and take a crowded bus for seven hours to the capital.

Dear god, from Haiti

Under the cover of night, we arrived in Port-au-Prince, greeted with hugs and Kreyol welcomes by Yoleine's family and friends. Before a treacherous drive to Leogane, we drove to the family home of Marjorie, who is Haitian-American, living in Connecticut. I rode to their home with her father. He spoke no English, yet we shared polite conversation in my broken French—which bears no comparison to Kreyol's musicality, eloquence, and elegance. Marjorie's father was a clean-cut gentleman, about 60 years of age. He was nattily-dressed in white, silken, short-sleeve collared shirt and off-white khaki pants.

Their home in the heart of Port-au-Prince was undamaged, though everything around them for miles seemed to have collapsed. Before facing the cross of corruption and catastrophe, we broke bread together: a Kreyol communion of plantains, rice and beans, chicken, and yuca. We gave thanks that your hand kept this house standing.

But god, you spared nothing else. Port-au-Prince is flattened. Piles upon piles of rubble and devastation cover a landscape dotted with palm, mango, and coconut trees. Among lush mountains and sugarcane fields, human and dog alike scavenge through concrete and twisted metal for a morsel. The stench of death and sewage were overwhelming as we dodged autos, tent cities, survivors, relief workers, and farm animals through the winding roads of refuge. We ran over a pig that, having seen enough, leapt in front of our vehicle. Night still hid most of the destruction, but our headlights momentarily exposed the biblical proportions of your damage. Miles upon miles of crooked houses, shattered concrete, and hundreds of thousands of people living on the streets.

On the outskirts of the city, and just before Leogane, we arrived at the tent city of Mon P'tit Village. On the Neges Foundation's land, there is a sturdy main house, a majestic gazebo, a community garden, a small domestic animal farm, and a soccer field. A rock's throw away from the main house in both directions, there are over 200 families—including some 500 children and at least 30 orphans—living on a field in white tents from France (the least they could do), which glowed with candles and fires. It was at first picturesque, then grotesque upon reflection.

Over the noise of a temperamental generator, I managed a few French pleasantries with Jean Marie, the resident naturalist. He then showed me to the two-bedroom tent that I would share with my colleague Lisel, a retired Ethical Culture clergy leader.

Awakened by an aggressive rooster's crow, I rose and made my way to the camp, longing for coffee and cigarettes. (Our addictions follow us everywhere.) As I arrived at the opening of the barbed-wire fence, I was greeted by Jean Marie, who seems to be everywhere at once. I told him I needed coffee and made the smoking gesture for cigarettes. He directed me down to the center of the camp. There, a woman was squatting before a makeshift charcoal-burning stove boiling my fix of caffeine. To her visible annoyance, I would return several times during the day. (I didn't find cigarettes until late that night.)

Dear god, from Haiti

As the sun began to crease the sky, the camp came alive. Children and adults—but mostly women—began their short trek to the water supply set up by the Spanish Red Cross behind the house. In the midst of misery, these folks took pride in keeping good hygiene; in the bright morning sun with a cup of water, men, women, and children brushed their teeth and washed their often-half-naked bodies behind their tents. They swept in front of their tents, singing songs. Mon P'tit Village is the Haitian spirit alive—bruised, but not broken.

Our task for the day was to dig holes for new toilets and unclog the only two on site. When we arrived there was one working toilet; we built three and dug holes for nine more. Peter, a Brit from York and a Volunteer for Peace, was our taskmaster. In his quirky cockney accent, he directed us to dig a new hole for the port-a-potty that was not yet overflowing with excrement, dig a second hole for the extra excrement to fill a wheelbarrow with dirt to cover the remaining excrement from the old port-a-potty hole.

The hole-digging had to be precise. The water-table was two and a half meters deep. If we dug more than a meter, it would contaminate the water supply for the entire community. Well water was the only consistent water supply in the community, since the water delivered by the Spanish Red Cross ran out after a few hours.

The meter measuring tape was our guide, the protector of these people's water. Lanai, a self-proclaimed positivist, helped to change us into our disaster relief haz-mat get-ups.

We wore plastic gloves, a shiny light-blue plastic apron, lemongrass oil on our top lips, and medical masks left over from the swine flu scare. On the count of three, Jean Marie and a Haitian man moved the overflowing port-a-potty, while the rest of us shoveled the extra shit into the other and covered up what remained. Despite the lemongrass, the smell was awful—god-awful, god. We all gagged and heaved, but no one threw up except me, only a little, in my mask.

We repeated this drill the following day with two other members of our delegation—Trenton, a giant of a man, and Alissa, the horticulturalist (another self-proclaimed positivist). At the end of each task, I removed my mask and yelled, "Viva Haiti!" They all laughed and responded in kind: "Viva Haiti!"

This all happened before 10 am. It was time to bathe. I had to go to the well and dip for my bathing water. I did not know how to do what was so effortless for the children, so they taught me and laughed at my attempts. A white bucket was attached to a twine rope several meters long; after being lowered at a deliberate pace, a few tugs laid it on its side on top of the water. As it filled, it lowered itself into the water until I pulled it up. It took two dips to fill the ten-gallon paint bucket that was now my tub.

There is something deeply theological, god, about shoveling shit and going to the well. The grossness of it all situates our finitude in the face of the catastrophic. White, liberal paternalism and pity is simply intolerable—more disturbing than the misery in Haiti. The Left needs to shovel the people's shit and go to the living waters in the people's wells. There is no resorting to convenient platitudes. Words like solidarity and comrade seem cheap and arcane to me now; only sacrifice, covenant, and accompaniment suffice.

In the face of such horrendous material conditions and the absurd call to rebuild, non-material resources are necessary. The greatest forces against hegemony and disaster are organized hope and revolutionary joy. I turned to my faith—but not you, god. We sang songs of freedom given to me by my ancestors. Several times a day, I sat on the ground with large groups of children. "Repete apres moi?" I asked. "Oui," they responded, and we sang heaven down.

All in Leogane, I gonna let it shine

All in Leogane, I gonna let it shine

All in Leogane, I gonna let it shine

Let it shine, Let it shine, Let it shine!

All in Leogane, I hear freedom in the air

All in Leogane, I hear freedom in the air

All in Leogane, I hear freedom in the air

There must be a god somewhere...

At one point we needed to drive into Leogane proper to buy wood for a three-person toilet. Passing the UN helicopter staging area—guarded by Sri Lankan soldiers in a pasture with bulls—we turned the bend and saw several tent cities and a flattened concrete one. The Neges Foundation's school was slightly damaged, and the volunteer house across the street was destroyed.

Winding again through tragedy, our driver Eddy pointed out in Kreyol the sites of mass death. James translated. We arrived at the remains of Leogane's hardware store for the wood. The prices were marked up 800%. Peter was livid and walked off. James tells the Haitian owners our displeasure, and we headed to another place that would give us fair prices.

Each day, members of our delegation led groups of children in arts, games, and education. The community garden was restored, and a youth delegation cleaned the camp. Guthrie and Micah assisted at the soup kitchen and makeshift, two-hour school day for 200 children. There were 300 more on the waiting list. Our delegation brought some 35 large duffle bags of supplies that included gardening tools, dry food, toothpaste, and soap.

The Brooklyn Society for Ethical Culture raised money. Its children sent notes and school supplies. My contributions came from Deluxe Hair Gallery in Brooklyn and the Computer School in Manhattan. Glenn and Mike, of Deluxe, together with their largely-female clientele, donated what seemed to be hundreds of sanitary products. Computer School's middlers gave boxes of crayons.

My last night in Leogane, we held a memorial service. In preparation for the gathering, I put on my white clergy robe with an orange and green stole as my waist sash. Walking through camp, people greeted me, "Mon frere, mon frere." Children held my hand. I tried to explain that I was not Catholic, but it didn't matter—they still wanted me to bless them, and I obliged.

Under the fractured gazebo, reinforced by steel adjustable poles, Yoleine gingerly led the memorial service. She told them in her native tongue that you, god, did not do this to them—though I'm not so sure. She mourned, and declared that whether one practices Voodoo, or Catholicism, or both, we are all together now and need to build a community.

We sang freedom songs. Lisel preached that the international community of women was with them. And Jean, a dance professor, performed with the community's dance troop, and the audience of 300—mostly children—celebrated her for celebrating them in her body. Late into the night they danced to Haitian music, hip-hop, and Bob Marley.

Mon P'tit Village is tragicomic. Their tent village was clean thanks to an ever-evolving sanitation system. The community was safe because some of the troublesome young men were organized into a security team. The guardians, as I liked to call them, patrolled the camp at night. The hard liquor ban was working as well. James coordinated a census which accounted for every man, woman, and child. Each tent was marked with a number and divided into sections. Yet major food deliveries only happened once every eight days or so. Haiti is hellish, but the Devil hasn't had the last word—yet.

I know you like numbers because you dedicated an entire book to them in what is purported to be your word. So let me give you a few:

1.5 million homeless
30,000 died in Leogane
250,000 total dead
6,500 tent cities

Evidently you shared your version of the earthquake's cause with your envoy, Pat Robertson. (By the way, a deal with the Devil for my freedom is a deal I am willing to make.) If the recent tone of my sermons and this letter have not made it clear, let me say in no uncertain terms—I am pissed off at you, god. If you did this, you did very, very wrong.

However, I will not give you the pleasure or satisfaction of me quitting. Haiti is not a test of my faith, or the faith of the people of Haiti, for that matter. Our faith is shaken but steady. We are rebuilding in the shit and filth, but you are hiding. Haiti is not a test of our faith but a test of your grace. Show yourself.

Sincerely,
Rev. Osagyefo Uhuru Sekou

the good samaritan on wall street

An ecumenical group of clergy conducted a tender communion service at Occupy Boston. Supported by the generous heart of Harvard Divinity School students, we broke bread and served wine in the holiest of Christian rituals. This Eucharist table was the table of Jesus— defender of the poor. Hymns rang out in the crisp evening air. Thirty or so clergy in vestments and stoles strolled through the crowd, offering up the cup and bread of life. Each one us hear from believer and non believer alike. "Thank you." We simply responded with equal gratitude. "No, thank you."

While religious leaders have played a minor role in the Occupy movement, there is something deeply spiritual if not religious taking place. The task of the theologian in the time of Occupy Wall Street is to continue to raise the question of ultimate concern—what does it mean to be human? Fourteen million human beings in the United States are grappling with the most basic of human considerations—food and shelter—forcing an often aloof profession to deepen its vocational calling. Nuanced and at times interesting debates about the nature of god and the church are drowned out by the groans of hungry disheartened and disinherited folks. What must emerge from this crumbling empire and recalcitrant academy obsessed with specialization is the organic theologian.

Appropriating Antonio Gramsci's organic intellectual, the organic theologian is a scholar who cultivates strong roots in their community, working to maintain links between theology and local struggles connecting to the people and their experiences. She uses her position to articulate discourses that aid communities and congregations develop new modes of being just. The organic theologian does not exist outside of history but rather assesses and articulates moments when the divine is breaking into history through social movements.

The Occupy Wall Street Movement has sprouted on an unique contemporary landscape. The three branches of United States government are thoroughly controlled and supported by corporate interest. The current administration has received 16 million dollars in contributions from the securities and investment industry and appointed veterans of that same industry who facilitated the deregulation which culminated in a world wide economic crisis. Through international trade agreements and bank bailouts, Congress has served the interest of Wall Street. The Citizen United ruling of the Supreme Court afforded corporations the same rights has human beings thereby unleashing an ungodly amount of contributions to political campaigns. (President Obama is scheduled to raise one billion dollars for his re-election campaign.)

The media—the fourth estate—created to serve as the informative caretaker of the democracy—extols the virtues of the wealthy, demonizes the poor and those who protest on their behalf. And the dominant theological project in United States declares that wealth is a sign of favor from god. In this thorny political and theological terrain, Occupy Wall Street Movement has come to the public discourse in search of not only policies but meaning. The organic theologian must consider these holy acts as signs and wonders in the last days of the empire.

"Can anything good come out of the Occupy Movement?" is the question of pundit and politician alike. The greater question for the organic theologian is "What does it mean to human in the decaying democracy?" "How do we honor "the body and blood" of those arrested and beaten by the police?" "What is the measure of our reasonable service?"

In the tenth chapter of Luke, Jesus tells the now familiar story of the Good Samaritan. As the robbed one lay bleeding and broken, he is ignored by countrymen and clergymen as they passed by. He is then happened upon by a Samaritan. The Samaritan tends to the robbed one's wounds, insures his safety with a place to rest, and continues to make sure that the robbed one is well. Jesus says the Samaritan loved his god with all his heart, mind, and soul and his neighbor as himself, which is the sum of the god's law. One might consider it odd that Jesus would left up a Samaritan as the hero of this parable. Samaritans are outliers through out the Biblical narrative. From Genesis onward Samaritans are treated with contempt-- hated by the Jewish oppressed and Roman oppressor alike. They worshiped the wrong God and their religious practice considered illegitimate.

They tended to live on the outskirts of the city and keep to themselves. Yet somehow this maligned people bore witness the sum of Biblical authenticity according to Jesus in his parable. The action of the Samaritan is to allow God to reign.

Veteran organizers have lobbied the Occupy to streamline its message and elect a spokesperson. The media mocked their dress. Both have missed the gift of these public congregations of hope.   While politicians and the media have shielded bankers from real scrutiny, the Occupy folks have come to Wall Street to tend to the wounds of those who were robbed on the roadside of the American Dream.

While prosperity preachers continue to beat people over the head for the little money that they have and politicians blamed the fore closures on the jobless, these democratic Samaritans have come to their aid but simple being there.

The gift and genius of Occupy is that is places all progressive if not revolutionary issues on the table. Racial, environmental, gender, sexuality and food justice are seen as direct links to the economic inequality.   The Occupy folks are the incarnation of the life and legacy of Jesus of Nazareth. With a billionaire mayor shouting down Occupy Wall Street, we see the incarnation of Pontius Pilate, who presided over Jesus' crucifixion.

"You can not disturb the business of Wall Street" says one of the richest men in the world to debt ridden students, decorated veterans, the chronic homeless, and former members of the middle class. For this organic theologian such a proclamation is ungodly and unseemly. The incarnation of the Occupy movements serves a reminder of the embodied sacrifice that is Jesus of Nazareth. Occupy's very presence is a public witness—an elegant and eclectic revival ushering in the *zeitgeist der agape*.

obama and the prophetic traditon

Traditionally, African American intellectuals and activists have encountered the office of the President as outsiders with a nuanced understanding and repertoire of tactics including electoral brokerage, inside strategy and social protest (organized and rhetorical).

These tactics have been executed against "The White Man." The oppositional politic was the normative means of encountering the office of the Presidency and the deployment of fierce rhetoric was an accepted means of public engagement. Both the candidacy and presidency of Barack Obama are a disruption of that rhetorical and tactical tradition. The African American tradition of speaking truth to power has been complicated because that power is now embodied by "A Black Man."

This is a unique moment in American democracy. The white supremacist gaze in the United States demonized black bodies, subjected their intelligence and interrogated their national allegiance. Barack Obama's winning campaign called into question these deep seated notions that shaped U.S. public policy and perceptions.

Hence, the Obama presidency is an electoral and existential victory. The way in which African American people make meaning for themselves inside the American empire has been recast. There is a widely accepted narrative about Obama's election. While it is true that his presence in the White House is because of his intelligence, effective fundraising apparatus and sophisticated campaign machinery, the red carpets at the inaugural balls were soaked in the blood of martyrs.

The presidency of Barack Obama is a by-product of African Americans' 400 years of struggle for access to the democratic project called America. The President has often located himself in that tradition and trajectory. He has strategically trafficked in the prophetic rhetoric of the Civil Rights Movement and employed the homiletical rhythms of the black church. He has conveniently used these cultural signifiers in a way that is titillating to the national consciousness—linguistically embodying Black folks' quest for a more democratic society.

Moreover, Black folks take great pride in the presence of three generations of African Americans in the White House. The real image of a beautiful Black family beaming into the homes of all Americans has a deep impact on the psyche of the nation, and a denigrated people. There is a collective desire on the part of African Americans to protect and shield their existential idol-President Barack Hussein Obama. This is a new space in U.S. history—racial and collective national memory. The right wing backlash, contemptible treatment, legislative obstructionism, and flat out disrespect consistently directed at the President and the First Family only serve to reinforce this protective existential and racial logic.

However, there is a counterpoint to this protectionist logic. Based on the criterion set forth by the African American freedom struggle, there is an expectation beyond physical and psychic symbolism. There must be public policy to reflect the very tradition that the President uses and benefited from in his rise to power. Is it inappropriate to have this expectation of the President Barack Obama? Is it appropriate for black folks to levy a critique and action against a black man in the White

House? Or must black leadership focus on defending the President from racist attacks?

The protectionist logic combined with the ultra conservative Republican Party has circumscribed the political vision of the vast majority of African Americans. The logic goes that criticism of the President is tantamount to supporting ultra conservative politics. Regardless of his legislative record, African Americans will vote for him in record numbers. This electoral allegiance is not a negotiating tool, but, rather, an existential duty. The protectionists cheapen any critical conversation about the President's agenda.

The only legitimate engagement is an insider strategy—access to the White House and supporting the administration's agenda at all cost. Accordingly, organized and rhetorical protests are, vehemently, dismissed. In this formulation, the aforementioned questions remain unanswered. The improvised electoral options guarantee that the President will not have to provide any substantive policy response to underemployment, unemployment, foreclosures, quality public education, expanding prison industrial complex and affordable housing—all of which affect African Americans, disproportionately. This makes him no different than any other president. Hence, he should be treated as such.

Every president since Abraham Lincoln has had to contend with an organized and rhetorical protest—the prophetic tradition. This tradition has always focused on the nation's treatment of the most vulnerable citizens— the least of these. Under the prophetic gaze, politicians have either been celebrated or rebuked. Fredrick Douglass and the abolitionists supported the Underground Railroad and offered stern public rebukes of Abraham Lincoln for not ending slavery. A. Phillip Randolph and the broader labor movement marched and chastised Franklin D. Roosevelt until the creation of the New Deal. Martin Luther King, Jr. and the Civil Rights Movement pressured and protested the Kennedy and Johnson administration into the passage of Civil Rights and the Great Society legislation.

King once remarked that electoral politics are thermometers—measuring political climate; social protests and movements are thermostats—setting political climate. Organized and rhetorical protests have set the climate for an effective insider strategy and subsequent electoral allegiance in the voting booth. Prophetic rhetoric and organized rage have created the context for the passage of public policy that improves the quality of life for the least of these. The contemporary political climate is such that there are very limited possibilities for progressive social policies to emerge from the administration, itself. A recalcitrant Congress, a right of center Democratic Party and two decades of neo-liberal policies require that the President serve a right of center agenda which has been at odds with the prophetic tradition and the needs of the most vulnerable.

Hence, African American leadership can not go it alone. The challenges facing democracy are nothing less that the retraction of the promise of the Civil Rights Movement, dismantling of the Great Society, and reversal of the New Deal—let alone an ever expanding prison and military industrial complex. The grand tradition of fiery prophetic rhetoric must remain connected to social movements. In order to shift the political discourse and create the conditions for progressive policy, a new multi- racial and multi- issue coalition has to emerge. Rhetorical protest must be matched with mass organizing.

gays are the new niggers

Those who declare "Gay is the New Black" have outraged intellectuals, religious leaders, and politicians inside the black community. They have outraged, for instance, Rev. Irene Monroe, who identifies three cardinal sins of whiteness plaguing the gay-marriage movement: 1) exploiting black suffering and experiences to legitimate its own; 2) rallying against heterosexist oppression while remaining silent on its own white-skin privilege; 3) appropriating the content of the black civil rights movement but discarding the historical context. Rev. Monroe is right. If there is to be a black-and-gay coalition, it will have to listen to her.

But it will also have to remember Bayard Rustin. Rustin, an openly gay black man, helped introduce Gandhian nonviolence to the African-American civil rights movement. His pacifism landed him in jail for refusing to participate in World War II. He was part of the first Freedom Rides in 1947, helped to found the Congress for Racial Equality, and was National Field Secretary for the Fellowship of Reconciliation.

Rustin was among the most famous advocates of Gandhian nonviolence in the 1930s and 1940s, and the Mahatma once summoned him to a conference in India. Beginning with the Montgomery Bus Boycott, he served as key adviser to Martin Luther King, Jr., giving him the chance to train Dr. King in the philosophy of nonviolence as a way of life.

However, Rustin's sexuality was not without controversy or consequence in the civil rights movement.

Under the cover of night in the trunk of a car, he was unceremoniously evacuated from Montgomery because a reporter threatened to expose Rustin's sexuality and past communist affiliation in the press.

Worried that his presence could hurt the bus boycott, King and Rustin agreed that it would be best if Rustin left town. Still, Rustin continued to advise King. He designed the organizational structure of the Southern Christian Leadership Conference and was the main fundraiser for the organization in its early stages.

When King decided to call a march on the 1960 Democratic Convention, the party dispatched Congressman Adam Clayton Powell to stop it. Powell manufactured a sexual relationship between King and Rustin, telling King that he was going to leak the story to the press if he didn't back down from his plans to march. King relented and Rustin resigned.

Nevertheless, as a seasoned veteran in nonviolent philosophy and direct action, Rustin was tapped to plan the 1963 March on Washington. In an interview, noted labor leader and march organizer A. Philip Randolph called Rustin "Mr.-March-on-Washington." In the weeks before, however, Strom Thurmond took the Senate floor to denounce Rustin's leadership and, with it, the civil rights movement as a whole. He gave a 45-minute speech, presenting pages upon pages about Rustin's activism and his arrest for having sex with two men in car in a California park and called Rustin a "communist, draft-dodger, and homosexual."

Gays are the New Niggers

As news of Rustin's arrests continued to surface, particularly the arrest for "moral indecency," there were calls for him to withdraw from planning the Washington march. Although the platform that launched Dr. Martin Luther King and the modern civil rights movement onto the world stage was orchestrated by an openly gay black man.

The march he helped organize would create the context for the passage of the Civil Rights Act in 1964 and the Voting Rights Act a year later, he was still villainized for his sexual orientation. In spite of the pressure, Randolph, King, and the other civil rights leaders—both in the press and behind closed doors—expressed their utmost confidence in Rustin, and he continued to lead the day-to-day organizing.

Bayard Rustin's authority to speak on the convergence of gay rights and civil rights is indisputable. He helped build the civil rights movement and suffered for being a gay man at the same time. Rustin's 1986 speech, "The New Niggers Are Gays" insists on the connection between gay rights and civil rights:

> Today, blacks are no longer the litmus paper or the barometer of social change. Blacks are in every segment of society and there are laws that help to protect them from racial discrimination. The new "niggers" are gays. ... It is in this sense that gay people are the new barometer for social change. ... The question of social change should be framed with the most vulnerable group in mind: gay people.

To say that gays are the new niggers is not to say that black oppression has disappeared. The claim that black folks are fully enfranchised and free is simply not true.

Stark racial and economic disparities continue to exist in the United States, regardless of who is in the White House.

Legislative onslaughts and public disdain against queer folks invites them into the community of niggers. By carrying the racial epithet beyond race, Rustin insists that blacks and queers share a common quest to save democracy. He calls us to look critically at the ways in which racism and heterosexism are two heads on the same devil.

In the essay "From Montgomery to Stonewall," Rustin continues to unearth the common roots of civil rights and gay rights. The Stonewall Inn in Greenwich Village, New York had been raided frequently by the New York City police for being a gay bar. But on June 28, 1969, a "routine" raid turned into a riot. Black, brown, and white folks—lesbian, gay, queer, and in drag—began to fight back against the systematic persecution, mocking and attacking the police. Supporters of the Stonewall patrons gathered outside in solidarity.

News reports and eyewitness accounts say that folks in the streets began to sing, "We shall overcome!" Soon after, all hell broke loose. Police, Stonewall patrons, and their supporters engaged in a brawl. That night, black and white queer folks were beaten together as niggers. Reality and metaphor should not be lost to one another. For Rustin, the events at Stonewall are part of a protest tradition in line with women's rights, civil rights, and anti-war demonstrations:

That was the beginning of an extraordinary revolution, similar to the Montgomery Bus Boycott in that it was not expected that anything extraordinary would occur As in the case of the women who left the Russian factory and in the case of Rosa Parks who sat down in the white part of the bus, something began to happen, people began to protest. They began to fight for the right to live in dignity, the right essentially to be one's self in every respect, and the right to be protected under law. In other words, people began to fight for their human rights. Gay people must continue this protest.

For oppressed communities around the world, the civil rights movement is a model for their unique and particular struggles. Although geography, pigmentation, class, religion, and capacity to self-organize may differ, they hold in common the structures of relegation and resistance. The police of conservative, racist, and homophobic forces wield literal and legislative billy clubs.

The absence of the word "slavery" in the Constitution is telling. 20% of would-be citizens were not worthy of naming in most sacred text of American civil religion. For another two centuries, this silencing of black human beings would continue to haunt American democracy. 600,000 people died in war as the nation came to grips with its silence.

It would take almost another century for the nation to hear the voices of the descendants of slaves in their cry for full enfranchisement. W.E.B. Du Bois noted that "the gift of black folks" to the democracy is that they appropriated the very terms of American democracy's sacred texts. The original intent of the Founding Fathers was not the enfranchisement or acknowledgment of the full humanity of black people, but black people called them to task for their words.

The black freedom struggle understood the Declaration of Independence and the Constitution as both the standard of and aspiration to what it means to be fully human on American soil. While their experiences were not the same as those of white Anglo-Saxons who were rejecting over-criminalization, religious intolerance, and British taxation without representation, African Americans shared the desire to be free and full citizens in the new democracy. The "niggers" took the language of democracy as the terms of their liberation.

The evangelization of slaves was intended to make African Americans docile and obedient, but they learned to read the Bible with a hermeneutic of suspicion. Whites, after all, had used scripture to justify slavery. The story of the cursing of Ham by Noah and Saint Paul's command that "slaves be obedient to your masters" were staples in the slave master's theology.

The slaves responded by seeing themselves as children of Israel who needed to be delivered from bondage. They learned to appropriate the experience of biblical Jews as America had appropriated the vision of itself as the new Zion. Their spirituals are rich religious texts, describing a liberating theology. "Over my head I hear freedom in the air … there must be a God somewhere," they sang, and "Oh Freedom over me/Before I be slave I'll be buried in my grave/and go home to my Lord and be free!"

Gays are the New Niggers

Bayard Rustin, a Quaker, recorded albums of songs like these to raise money for the civil rights movement and other social justice causes. He used the spirituals to hold the anti-democratic demons at bay. Slaveholders intended the Bible and Christianity to sanction their oppression and pacify slaves in their oppression.

But black folks took hold of the biblical narrative and the sacred civic texts to affirm the right to be free. They read the Bible in one hand and the Constitution in the other. On a cross constructed with these two existential beams, the bodies of black people and their allies hung for the remission of the founders' original sin.

The historical and contemporary experiences of black and queer folks not are the same. They are different—but not dissimilar. Naming (faggot and nigger), vigilante violence/hate crimes (Matthew Shepard and Emmett Till), legislative disenfranchisement (Plessy vs. Ferguson and Prop. 8), hyper-sexualized stereotypes, and housing and employment discrimination have been used to undermine the humanity of both groups. And, for both, much of it has been done and justified by religion.

Their common lot can be described as simultaneous: a historical and contemporary use of oppressive mechanisms and meanings that are mirrored over time and space that produce similar intended outcomes of discriminations experienced by historically othered people. Oppressive forces across discriminatory categories (e.g. race, class, gender, sexual orientation, age, and immigration status), deploy similar brutal methods. They must be answered with a common cause.

Their simultaneous situatedness carries a moral obligation to compare struggles and stories, to forge an existential identification between the oppressed groups. In the past, black folks were the chief victims of moral outrage and political warfare; queer folks share in the ire.

Rustin, however, places the burden of proof on the queer community. There are responsibilities that come to those who claim to be oppressed. Indifference to the suffering of other human beings cannot be a part of one's own struggle, he insists. The queer community cannot work toward justice for itself alone. It must, self-critically, reject all forms of prejudice.

Rustin writes that a society that denies school children food will never grant gay rights. By the same logic, a society that rejects universal healthcare, embraces preemptive war, and houses more black men in prison than in college will never grant queer folks their God-given rights or their rights as democratic citizens. To share in the hateful legacy of "nigger" requires generosity on the part of black people. We must be freely giving of the gift we have given democracy for over four centuries.

In the same manner that Rustin and others marched and were beaten for everybody's democracy, we must continue to extend the hand of freedom and the history of hope to the queer community. We have so much to teach: how to be persecuted but not forsake our democratic values, how to be cast down but not out, and how to meet legislative setbacks with existential victories.

Gays are the New Niggers

A dreadful word with so much ugly history is the very window through which we can begin to see each other's humanity. All niggers—historical and contemporary—must join forces to achieve freedom for all. Rustin places a moral challenge on those in the struggle: "Every indifference to prejudice is suicide because, if I don't fight all bigotry, bigotry itself will be strengthened and, sooner or later, it will return on me."

queering democracy and christianity

A few years ago, I interviewed to serve as the Senior Minister of a church in the Bronx. I was excited by the very idea of serving as a pastor in the poorest congressional district in the country, plus the "Boogie Down" is the birth place of Hip Hop. Surrounded by the thick cloud of pollution that is the air and decaying housing while being serenaded by blaring sirens and Nuyorican accents, the century old white stone church stood in all of its majesty.

I rang the door bell. A tall stately woman with a graceful all gray hair cut invited me into the small conference room. The Pastoral Search committee was waiting—five "little old ladies" dressed in their Sunday morning best on a weekday evening. Directed to the empty chair at the far end of the room, I greeted each one of them with a hand shake and slight genuflection. I anxiously took my seat at the head of the table. "Mother," a small, dainty, if not fragile, yet dignified elder, sat directly across the reckoning table.

After a softball question from the tall woman who initially welcomed me, "Mother" came-a-swinging. With disdain in her voice she asked, "Reverend Sekou, what do you think of gay marriage?!"

Taking a deep breath, I hesitated. In the silence she forcefully reminded me, "And you know what the Bible says!"

With head bowed in deference to my elder I said, "Mother, the Bible says, women be silent in the church."

The committee nodded in recognition, as I continued to seal my fate. "You got around that, didn't you?"

"Yes," they all said.

"Bible says 'slave be obedient to your masters.'"

"Yes, yes," they perked up.

"We got around that."

"This is true," Mother conceded.

"I think we can get around this," I said.

"Black folks looked at the text that affirmed their humanity and rejected the text that did not. Do not gay folks have the right to do the same? In fact, I would argue that the Bible does an amazing job arguing for justice for all. Did you know that there are over 3,000 references to poverty and the poor in the Bible?"

They nodded in collective astonishment and deployed the cultural idiom, "Umph."

Taking it up a notch, I leaned forward and preached, "And it really makes God mad. In the Bronx, with the highest rates in poverty, per capita imprisonment, HIV/Aids cases, and asthma in New York City, should we not be focused on that work? I am doing what you taught me, 'Mother.' Black women like you taught me that wherever folks are catching hell I gotta show up. Gay folks are catching hell so I gotta show up. Black folks should not ever be part of denying anyone rights."

Collecting my emotions, I sat back. The committee agreed to send my name to the broader congregation to be voted up after a Sunday morning sermon. This story does not end perfectly, though. I did not become the pastor of that church. I lost the congregation vote, 16-8. It seems, in that case, I was only able to convince the five "little old ladies" and three living husbands. I persuasively converted five older African American church ladies and leaders. They left that interview believing that gay marriage was consistent with their own sense of theological agency and the African American freedom struggle.

Bible verses are often cited as the god-given admonition against gay marriage, same gender loving, and as the penultimate guide for relationships. First, there is the ever popular Old Testament Leviticus 20:13, "If a man lies with a male as he lies with a woman, both of them have committed an abomination." In the New Testament, the Apostle Paul poses and answers questions concerning the unrighteous. He writes in his first letter to the church at Corinthians:

> Do you not know that the unrighteous will not inherit the kingdom of God? Do not be deceived, neither fornicators, nor idolaters, nor adulterers, nor homosexuals, nor sodomites, nor thieves, nor covetous, nor drunkards, nor revilers, nor extortioners will inherit the kingdom of God.

In this same letter Paul offers some very clear instructions for women. "As in all the congregations of the saints, women should remain silent in the churches. They are not allowed to speak, but must be in submission, as the Law says. If they want to inquire about something, they should ask their own husbands at home; for it is disgraceful for a woman to speak in the church."

Paul also writes to the church in Ephesus and encourages, "[s]laves, be obedient to them that are [your] masters according to the flesh, with fear and trembling, in singleness of your heart, as unto Christ." As signification of their faithfulness, the text demands obedience of women and slaves to those "placed over them" and calls same gender loving an "abomination."

Faced with an oppressive Christianity that justified their bondage and beating, they ingested scriptures that fed their ontological desire to be liberated. They, in turn, rejected texts that were counter to their beingness. In its plainest sense, "queer" means to be at odds with the prevailing society. Because of these shared themes of oppression, being black is queer and being queer is black—signifying that to be black/queer is to be at odds with the democracy.

Through the blood stained freedom struggle of the small, but prophetic, church, black folks queered democracy and Christianity, changing the oppressive systems into symbols of liberation for all to behold. Perhaps, then, if queer folks use this hermeneutic of suspicion, they can also reclaim the liberating promise of Christianity and democracy. Linkages can made between the African American struggle for civil rights and the struggle for the rights of queer folks. Black folks queered democracy and Christianity. The problems of appropriation and religion have been negotiated by black folks for four centuries in the United States. That's why other oppressed groups—in this case, queers—come to see black folks as models for what it means to be a self-actualized people confronting discrimination. The civil rights movement set the stage for the queer rights movement because of its power and grace when confronted with the ugliness of prejudice, hatred, and violence. Black and queer folk share in a common struggle against discrimination. Coretta Scott King, noted activist in her own right, makes the connection. Speaking at a National Gay and Lesbian Task Force gathering, Mrs. King articulated a common struggle between civil and queer rights.

> I say "common struggle" because I believe very strongly that all forms of bigotry and discrimination are equally wrong and should be opposed by right-thinking Americans everywhere. Freedom from discrimination based on sexual orientation is surely a fundamental human right in any great democracy, as much as freedom from racial, religious, gender, or ethnic discrimination.

The passage of legislation that denies gay marriage and adoption restricts democratic expansion instead of expanding democratic access. Such actions are counter to nearly two centuries of small yet vocal religious social movements to expand democracy. The religious precedent of democratic expansion mandates that such religious calls for restriction have no place in public policy.

Equally, there are religious denominations that ordain queer folks and administer the sacrament of marriage to same sex couples. The first sentence of the First Amendment of the Constitution states that: "Congress shall make no law respecting an establishment of religion, or prohibiting the free exercise thereof[.]" Given the religious dogma used to justify anti-gay marriage legislation, state laws and a proposed Constitutional amendment are a violation of the First Amendment of the Constitution because they impose one form of religion over another.

The repressive forms of religion, such as those citing same-sex relationships as Biblical abomination, or encouraging the enslaved to be obedient to their masters, have only served to undermine the democracy—and these restrictions cut against the religious precedent for democratic expansion. In concurrence with the constitutional formulation, the Iowa Supreme Court struck down the passage of a ban against gay marriage. The Iowa decision privileges democratic expansion over religious restriction:

> As a result, civil marriage must be judged under our constitutional standards of equal protection and not under religious doctrines or the religious views of individuals. This approach does not disrespect or denigrate the religious views of many Iowans who may strongly believe in marriage as a dual-gender union, but considers, as we must, only the constitutional rights of all people, as expressed by the promise of equal protection for all. We are not permitted to do less and would damage our constitution immeasurably by trying to do more. A new distinction based on sexual orientation would be equally suspect and difficult to square with the fundamental principles of equal protection embodied in our constitution. This record, our independent research, and the appropriate equal protection analysis do not suggest the existence of a justification for such a legislative classification that substantially furthers any governmental objective.

Consequently, the language in Iowa Code section 595.2 limiting civil marriage to a man and a woman must be stricken from the statute, and the remaining statutory language must be interpreted and applied in a manner allowing gay and lesbian people full access to the institution of civil marriage.

Religious discourse in public policy must be about the expansion of democratic opportunity. Marriage grants over 1,300 civil rights to its participants, including property rights and end of life decisions. This must be extended to queer folk as part of the democratic expansion. To deny civil rights is to cut against the grain of both the best of the Black Church, and the prophetic tradition that has served to make America more democratic nation.

exiles in the kingdom

"Yo fam, you on the block? Watch out 4 green VW van. Trident just jammed me." Mark Duggan, a 29-year-old father of four, sent that text to his mates and family at 6:00pm on Thursday, August 4th, 2011. Semone Wilson, Mark's partner, frantically tried to find out the state of the father of her three children. Mark Duggan was born and reared on The Farm—Broadwater Farm Estate, a storied public housing community in Tottenham, North London.

A week after his shooting which sparked riots in Tottenham and across England, I arrived on The Farm. Mark's friend, Gary is a small shopkeeper on The Farm. Shocked into quietude, he fumbled with his Blackberry, head hung in grief as he showed me one of the last text messages Mark Duggan would ever send.

At 6:07 on that fateful Thursday evening, Gary and others replied to the text but got no response. Around 6:15pm London Metropolitan Police stopped a silver Toyota Estima minicab on Ferry Lane near Tottenham Hale tube station. The pre-planned police action was to arrest Mark, the minicab passenger.

According to police sources, Duggan was an alleged drug dealer on his way to avenge, Kelvin Easton, who had been stabbed to death the previous March. The operation was being conducted by three distinct units of the London Metropolitan Police Service: Operation Trident—a unit specializing in black-on-black gun crime; Public Order Operational Command, intelligence gathering unit; and the Specialist Firearms Command Unit (CO19), highly trained marksmen providing firearms capacity to the unarmed

Metropolitan Police Service. The moments between police stopping the mini cab and Duggan's shooting are the most controversial. Minutes after the traffic stop, Mark's younger brother Marlon got a call from an eyewitness saying that Mark has been shot by police near the Tottenham Hale tube station—less than two miles from The Farm's "Frontline," the hangout spot in front of Gary's store. Rushing to the scene at the tube station, Marlon Duggan encountered several police.

According to friends and family, Marlon was told that his brother had been rushed to The Royal London Hospital in East London. Marlon called Semone who had received Mark's text as well, and told her that he thought Mark was shot by the police. Meeting Marlon at hospital, they were told that Mark was not there. They should go back to Tottenham Hale Station.

Semone, fearing the worst, rushed back to the scene. After showing police Mark's birth certificate and pictures of Mark on her phone, she was allowed to cross the yellow tape. After describing tattoos of their children that adorned his body, the police still refused to tell her if he had been shot, even as Mark Duggan's lifeless body lay under a sheet at the scene. "They would not tell me if it was Mark, who had been shot but I just knew." The 29-year-old, sadly, remembered. "I just waited around two or three hours and they did not tell me that it was Mark."

A member of The Independent Police Complaint Commission (IPCC), entrusted with conducting an objective investigation into deaths involving police, gave Semone a phone number. The IPCC official told her to go home, get some rest and someone would contact her. With only a gut feeling, Semone returned home and was shocked at the news reports. The British Broadcasting Company (BBC) reported that there was a shoot-out in which a police officer was wounded and Mark Duggan was fatally shot. *The Daily Mail*, Britain's second largest newspaper, publishing a similar account:

> Mark Duggan, 29, was in a car being followed by police during a covert operation...But Duggan, a known offender from London's notorious Broadwater Farm Estate, became aware that he was being followed and opened fire on the officers. He shot the officer from Scotland Yard's elite firearms squad CO19 in the side of his chest with a handgun. Armed officers shot the gunman dead seconds later.

Rupert Murduch's *London Times* headlined "Policeman cheats death after bullet hits radio during London gunfight." Stafford Scott, a 51-year-old community activist dating back to the Broadwater Farm Riots of 1985, said the Duggan family believed the bullet lodged in the police officer's radio is the bullet that went through Mark's bicep. Shaun Hall, Mark's brother told me that the gun slinging gangster reports about Mark were, "Rubbish." Neither Semone nor Stafford could say for sure whether Mark was in possession of a weapon at the time of his death, but they were confident that he wouldn't use a weapon against the cops. "I knew straightaway that it was not right. He was a runner. He would have run from the police," Semone hoped. Stafford insisted in no uncertain terms that Mark was not "mad" enough to shoot at the police.

Three days after riots began, the official IPCC report stated only two shots were fired and that there was no shoot out. An unnamed officer from the Specialist Firearms Command United fired two shots from a Heckler & Koch machine pistol, killing Mark Duggan. One bullet fatally struck Mark in the chest. A second round went through his right bicep. He was pronounced dead on the scene at 6:41pm.

The Forensic Science Service was commissioned by the IPCC to conduct tests on a bullet that was found lodged in a police officer's jacket radio. Initial findings, pending DNA results, indicate that the bullet was police issue. A converted BBM 'Bruni' with a "bulleted cartridge" was discovered at the scene wrapped in a sock. The Italian-made starter pistol which was modified to fire live ammunition is illegal under the British Firearms Act. "There were no finger prints on the (Bruni) gun." according to Semone, which means there is no way to verify if the gun belonged to Mark. In an odd, unprecedented, if not illegal procedure, the police allowed the minicab in which Mark was a passenger to be moved, shortly, thereafter, the cab was returned to the scene. Shaun wondered aloud if the pistol found at the scene "was planted by the police."

The understandably unnerved minicab driver who picked Duggan up was unavailable for public comment. Through an anonymous source, the cab driver has communicated to the family that what happened to Mark "did not have to happen."

The IPCC report affirmed Shaun, Stafford and Semone's confidence in Mark: "At this stage there is no evidence that the handgun found at the scene was fired during the incident." The officer whose radio helped him "cheat death" was taken to Homerton Hospital, examined and released the same night.

And although London has one of the most extensive public surveillance systems in the world, the closed-circuit camera footage that could clear up the family's lingering questions has yet to be released. Moreover, the media scandal involving newspaper owned by Rupert Murdoch cast a distrustful shadow over the police driven media story concerning Mark's death.

The lack of information from the police and the circulating rumors that Mark was assassinated only served to stir the emotions of Mark's friends, family, and the Black community in London. One eyewitness, who worked near the Tottenham Hale tube station, told the London *Evening Standard*:

> I came around the corner and saw about six unmarked police cars cornering a people carrier near a bus stop. I heard the police shout something like 'Don't move' and I saw them drag the driver out of the car... About three or four police officers had both men pinned on the ground at gunpoint. They were really big guns. And then I heard four loud shots. The police shot him on the floor.

The Economist quoted a mother in Hackney saying "People here are angry because of that boy the police executed in Tottenham." Four hundred people gathered outside the Duggan family home that night to pay their respects the night Mark died—night after night they returned to found out what really happened. London Metropolitan Police Service did not contact Semone or Mark's parents. In cases where a civilian is killed by police officers, it's standard police operating procedure to dispatch a Family Liaison Officer (FLO) to serve as a mediator between police and the family of the deceased. The FLOs have been quite busy over the last two decades.

According to Inquest, a U.K.-based nonprofit that provides services to the families of people killed by police, over 1,400 Britons died in police custody between 1990 and 2011. A U.K. police officer has never been convicted of the wrongful death of a civilian. Just this past May, the legendary UK dancehall artist Smiley Culture died while in police custody. Arrested during a raid on his house, officers claimed that Smiley stabbed himself to death, although community leaders and artist's family rejects the suicide story.

Instead of useful information from the police or facts from the media, Mark Duggan's family ran up against a barricade of silence and received a barrage of labels plastered upon the lifeless body of their beloved—notorious, gangster, crack dealer, thug, drug lord. Yet Mark had no criminal convictions.

To break the silence of the IPCC or the police, Semone called the IPCC demanding answers. Early on Saturday, August 6, the IPCC made arrangements for fourteen of Mark's friends and family to come to Haringey Mortuary for the viewing and identification of the body. Seeing Mark's body laying there with two bullet wounds only fueled the family and The Farm's desire for answers from Scotland Yard. Frustrated and grieving, Mark's friends and family began to organize. Around 5pm on Saturday, August 6, forty or so family and community members peacefully marched from the Farm to the Tottenham Police station. "It was a peaceful protest. We carried signs saying, 'WE WANT JUSTICE'", a dazed Semone recalled on a bench on The Farm.

When facing a crisis most communities turn to tried and proven leaders. In Broadwater Farm that man is tall, dark, and handsome Stafford Scott. As a central figure in the Broadwater Farm Riots in 1985, Stafford knows firsthand the outcome of police misconduct against a resident of The Farm.

On October 5, 1985 a young black man, Floyd Jarrett, was stopped and arrested by police for a motor vehicle registration violation. Later that day four police officers raided his home in search of drugs. Floyd's sister Patricia was in the apartment during the raid. She said that a police officer shoved their 49-year-old mother Cynthia Jarrett, who had a heart attack and instantly died. Just a week before, in similar circumstances as Mrs. Jarrett's, the police shot and paralyzed Dorothy Groce, an unarmed Black woman in Brixton. A riot popped off during a subsequent protest in front of the local police station.

On October 6, 1985, the day after Cynthia Jarrett's death, there was a small demonstration outside the Tottenham police station. Violence between police and protestors escalated. Returning to The Farm, the youth set up barricades and lit cars on fire, attacking police with bricks and homemade Molotov cocktails. According to eyewitnesses, while the officers were retreating, Officer Keith Blakelock broke rank, swung his baton at a rioter, missed and slipped—falling over a balcony. Straightaway, he was set upon by a machete wielding mob and suffered a horrific death.

The Haringey Council, the governing body of The Farm dispatched Stafford Scott to quell riots. At the time he was a youth worker who had been reared on The Farm. He admits he failed in that mission. Two days after the riot, Stafford's home was raided by armed police on suspicion that he was involved in Officer Blakelock's death. After roughing up his family, the police took Stafford into custody. At the police station, Stafford was stripped, searched, and forced to give hair, blood, and saliva for DNA samples. He was then released without being charged in connection to Officer Blakelock's death or the riots. Stafford and his family were later awarded a significant sum of damages from the London Metropolitan Police for the terrifying episode.

Walking though Tottenham with Stafford Scott felt like walking with Malcolm X in Harlem. Every few feet there was a call out to him: "Bless up." Random people would stop and thank him for his work. Stafford is their man against the Man. As we walked into his favorite Jamaican restaurant, Caribbean Spice, we encountered Michael Watson, a former world class boxer with slurred , who bore a remarkable resemblance to Muhammad Ali.

Stafford ordered a hefty bowl of fish soup. We settled into a table near the restaurant's kitchen. Another young man came in and interrupted our interview to say, "Big speech you give on Mark Duggan, Mon. Bless up." The fiercely eloquent Stafford placed his right hand over his heart and bowed his head, humbly whispering, "Bless up."

Fluidly moving between Jamaican patois and the Queen's English, the activist broke down how things unfolded on Saturday, August 6 in front of the Tottenham Police Station. "We had not received contact from the FLO. The police had not reached out to the family and refused to give them any answers," Stafford explained, sounding frustrated and flustered. "The community decided that three women would ask to speak with the most senior officer. We sent the women to be as non-threatening as possible."

Semone, her mother, Yvonne Hazelwood, and Mark's childhood friend Jenny ascended the steps of the police station. They requested to speak with the most senior officer. "I wanted to report a murder," Semone told the desk officer. With dismayed proper English, she continued, "The murder of Mark Duggan." The women were told that the police were handling the case and that they should step aside.

Luke Rabbito, a theatre director, lives directly across from the Tottenham Police station and had a bird's eye view of the peaceful gathering. Around 4pm Luke noticed a crowd forming at the police station. They carried signs that read: WE WANT JUSTICE! Frequently pointing with a boyish charm, Luke stood on the side walk and gave me a director's cut of the peaceful protest for Mark on August 6th:

> There were a group of friends and family about that started protesting outside the police station—about 40 or so. It was fairly peaceful, about three police officers present. About 20 minutes later, people laid down and blocked the street. The police began to redirect traffic. The only thing that kicked off was there was one guy passing through the

crowd and was given a shove by the police. He was just passing along and completely unconnected to the protest.

The crowd became increasingly impatient. "What do we want?" Justice! When do we want it? Now!" A Black police officer arrived in an unmarked car with a briefcase. He was promptly booed and went into the station. He came outside, again, attempted to address the crowd, but was chastised because he was not the senior officer. I told the police officer who came down that he would be responsible for whatever happens," Stafford recalled. "We did not want to be at the station after nightfall."As they continued to chant, the crowd grew agitated.

Concerned about the growing crowd, an approaching bus driver stopped, let off his passengers, took the keys and abandoned the double-decker bus on the road. About two hours after the police officer came down, Semone, her mother, and Jenny grew weary, and left the growing crowd. "After we waited for four hours we left with our group of about 100 and went back to The Farm," said Semone.

After two days of silence from the police department, four hours of peacefully gathering, and a steady diet of misinformation about Mark and the events surrounding his death, all hell broke loose shortly after 9pm. Their numbers swelled by Twitter and Facebook, the now unruly 400-plus crowd marched up High Road, the main thoroughfare in Tottenham. Riot police assembled, charged with protecting the Tottenham Police station. Targeting their rage, a number of young men unleashed upon two unmanned police cruisers with bottles, bricks, and stones. Then after some exchange between police and a 16-year-old-girl, a dozen or so off.

Judging by a YouTube clip, the scene was pure pandemonium, with officers dressed in all-black riot gear—plastic shields, helmets with face guards, and Billy clubs—standing over a teenage girl curled up in the fetal position and just beating her. One female onlooker screamed, "Look how they are dealing with her. It is a fucking girl!" Another unseen West Indian man shouted the most profane of Jamaican slurs, "*Bloodclaat*."

The sight of police beating a 16-year-old girl fuelled the riotous fire. The young men attacked police and torched the empty Double-Decker bus. In a furry of rage, store windows were broken out and the businesses looted for their goods. "It's 85 all over again!" Stafford told me, his eyes filled with tears, "They are doing to our boy what they did to us."

Watching helpless as Tottenham burned, Rowdy T, went to the lab. He dropped an eerie underground hit, *Riot Muzik*. Born on Broadwater Farm, Rowdy T knew Mark Duggan. Speaking from his Miami home, Rowdy T pointed out "This not the first time the police have done this. I had to speak on it". Accompanied by the sound of wood burning, *Riot Muzik* opens with Winston Churchill's voice, "You must never give in. Never Never give in". Rowdy T shouts out "North London, Tottenham, Mark Duggan, Rest In Peace." Pointing out the "war between the police and the streets," Rowdy calls for self-defense. Echoing Martin Luther King's Jr. claim that "riots are the language of the unheard." Rowdy T ripped the urgent track: "Loot something. . .We aren't scared/bust your gun because they don't hear our tears. "

In a reverse repeat of 1985 Brixton caught fire after Tottenham. Forty six other neighborhoods and cities in Britain soon burned. After bellowing smoke consumed Her Majesty's lair, the police would eventually apologize to the family for their handling of the case. By the time I arrived in London, the Kingdom was cleaning up the ashes and beginning to prosecute the thousands of people arrested during five days of rioting, looting, and arson from London to Bristol, the Midlands, and Northwest England.

I headed straight to Brixton, the center of Britain's Jamaican community, where the legendary poet and hip hop artist David J, the Vocal Pugilist, gave me a tour. He guided me to a makeshift shrine located directly in front of the Brixton police station. A tree covered in photos, candles, and flowers was dedicated to Ricky Bishop, a 25-year-old father of one.

Out of the blue David J spits a line about British police brutality: "Their eyeball coordination/is in synchroniz-ation/with the gun barrel's rotation/our grief is just paper work at the station." Ricky Bishop was a passenger in a car stopped in 2001 by police conducting a program known as "operation clean sweep." Detained but not arrested, he was beaten at the Brixton police station and died shortly thereafter in Kings College Hospital. The cause of death was ruled a misadventure" death. On cue David J, closed our pilgrimage to Ricky's shrine, "Stop and search, stop ya heart from beating / And search for a reason / to prevent you from breathing."

After surveying Brixton's looted shops we headed north to Tottenham. Making our way down High Road, I recognized the police station from worldwide accounts. The broken store windows were already boarded up; badly burned buildings secured by a wooden plank fences. The most devastated part of Tottenham was behind police barricades with Bobbies to boot.

We stopped and chatted with a record store owner. In a thick Jamaican accent, he gave us directions to The Farm. Broadwater Farm is a sprawling community set unto itself off a main street. To gain entry to the actual estate you have to go down a long street with trees on one side and a high brick wall on the other. Some young lads on bikes pointed us in the right direction.

Like most council estates, Britain's public housing is typically populated by ethnic minorities, and The Farm is heavily Jamaican. Cautiously meandering about, David, who was not pleased with my adventure, agreed that we should go over to the Frontline, a gathering spot area adjacent to Gary's little grocery store. Straightaway we were set upon by a dozen or so young men, all full of questions, some attempting to be menacing in their demeanor.

"Nigga, you ain't with no VIBE," barked Wan-Cee, the self-proclaimed Poet Laureate of the Farm. I showed them my assignment letter but that was not sufficient. Using his Iphone, Wan-Cee googled my name and found out that I am a pastor as well.

Showing the suspicious crowd internet pictures of me in clergy regalia they seemed to lighten up. After Gary asked us to move down away from the entrance of his store, the bespectacled "Pops" told the group to let us talk. Most refused to go on record by name and declined any video recording. Only one gentleman allowed me to record an audio interview. That was Lex, the "Big Mon" of the Farm who brandishes the unparalleled respect of little old ladies, wannabe thugs, Members of the Order of the British Empire, and Stafford Scott, alike. His rough and tough swagger is tempered by a joyous smile and generous spirit.

Lex gave a blow-by-blow of the events concerning Mark's death, much of the IPCC report confirmed. It was from Lex that I first heard about the bullet lodged in the officer's radio being from a police gun. "Mark laughed at the police and they shot him." Lex reported and others co-signed. They told me how the police came by and taunted them only hours after Mark was shot. Mark's mates said police made it their habit to ride by the Frontline to intimidate them.

Lex, graciously, invited me into his home—an immaculate townhouse with a well manicured back yard and tomato garden. In his dining room stood over the big 5-0 birthday cake that was never cut. "Me worst birthday ever". Lex turned 50 on the day that Mark was killed.

"Pops," who as a juvenile served 8 years behind bars for his role in the '85 riots, suggested that we come to the Nine Night—a Jamaica mourning ritual that traditionally spanned over nine nights to celebrate the life of the deceased. Well over one thousand people were on hand to bear witness to the life of another young black man that was taken by British police. People walked through the crowd soliciting funds to cover the food.

With Lex leading the way through to crowd, I saw Wan-Cee, gave him a fist bump arriving at the food table. Lex introduced me to Mark's sister Kay. I gave some flowers out of respect. She and other family and friends wore white t-shirts with a R.I.P. Mark featuring a large picture of Mark smiling on the front. The picture reminded me of a video that Lex showed me during my visit to his home. In the video, Mark was carrying the casket of his best friend, Kelvin Easton an up and coming rapper known as Smegz. He was stabbed through the heart, killed in a Tottenham nightclub in March 2011. Mark wore as white linen jacket that featured on the back a large picture with R.I.P. SMEGZ. Police sources say Mark was on his way to avenge SMEGZ death when he was shot by police.

Reggae music and heartfelt prayers saturated the community centre as the entire community grieved. Michelle Palmer Scott, Semone's sister hushed the crowd to bless the food. She lamented the death of Mark. Then, Michelle prayed heaven down with fire, "Oh, God help us bring justice for Mark. You know the truth. You know the police murdered Mark." The community center congregants reverberates "Jah, Praise Jesus, Hallelu-Jah!" And the prayer ended with a thousand voices. "Amen."

When Mark's alleged gang affiliation would come up folks rushed to his defense. Ileasha Wyndham, a very fashionable and very tall 28 year old, remembered as Mark was a shy funny guy. Born on The Farm, Ms. Wyndham, an operational and logistical accountant, was clear that "He was not a gangster." "He picked his son up every day and attended all of the games. Mark was a good and involved father", Clasford Stirling, director of Broadwater Farm football team, fondly remembered. "He was like a son to me," retorted the burly baritone honored by Queen Elizabeth. Kemani, Mark's ten year old son played football for Striling. A community pastor remembered a quiet and respectful Mark picking up his seven year old son, Kajuan from their after school program. Clasford understood that Mark was not a saint but "like most black youth who grow up, get in a little trouble and get criminalized."

At twenty-two Mark was held by police for possession of marijuana. The amount was so small—for personal use—that he was released with no criminal convictions. Clasford's own son was unjustly apprehended. The police were extremely, repentant after they realized that the young black man's father was a member of the Most Excellent Order of the British Empire. Stafford, Lex, Pops, and countless others told tales of being targeted by the police—often for nothing or minor offenses. At times leading to a self-fulfilling prophesy of criminality. "You get nicked for nothing you might as well do something", both Stafford and Lex shared at separate occasions.

On The Farm, I heard two consistent messages from several community members. First, Mark was not in a gang and secondly, they felt that the police were the biggest gang in London. This characterization of the police extended far beyond The Farm.

"You lots are the biggest gang/you think that badge makes you a bigger man?" MC Logic rhymed on "Mr. Officer. " Produced by Bars for Change, a Hip Hop organization working to bridge music and politics, the compilation track chronicles the history and contemporary experience of young people and police brutality. Logic name checks people who have died in police custody, "We believe you pigs, killed Smiley, Kingsley Burrell, Rickey Bishop, and Blair Peach/Until there is justice there'll be no peace"

Logic and DJ Snuff spoke with me at length on a longstanding hostility between young Black people in the police. Still rocking the mic, "The police operate in our communities without impunity," Logic sternly told me. "Every generation rebels against the police in the U.K.," the Belfast breed Snuff insisted with Irish ire. On July 1st, just 33 days before Mark was gunned down by police, Logic chaired a forum, "Who Polices the Police?" in Brixton. At the forum at Lambert Hall, Hip Hop artists and activists took up the relationship between young folks and the police in London.

The night before the funeral the Duggan's backyard was filled with the aroma of jerk chicken on the grill. Pamela and Bruno Duggan's modest two story house was a short drive from The Farm. Pictures of Mark, large and small, featuring his brilliant smile, graced the walls and shelves in the living room. His parents have begun to fray under the weight of it all. Bruno smiled and shook my hand with exhausted eyes—weakened by grief and terminal cancer. Pamela informed me that she was taking valium to help cope with the unbearable stress and grief. Marlon, Mark's youngest brother, was not much for talking.

Shaun —the chief spokesman for the family—had a dignified presence—impressing a member of Parliament. "The family remained so dignified throughout this whole ordeal," Baron Frank Judd, a member of the House of Lords, shared during our conversation at the ultra exclusive Royal Commonwealth Society.

The former president of Oxfam, the international anti-poverty organization, firmly believes that poverty, high unemployment, and poor community police relations were all contributors to the riots. Drawing in the air with his index fingers, "If you create a map of every community where there was riot there is a direct correlation to the level of poverty and depravation in that community."

In Tottenham, the first place to be set ablaze, 80.3 % of children living in poverty. The young black male community has been particularly hard hit by the global recession. An Institute for Public Policy Research report states unemployment rate for black British youth between the ages of 16 to 24 years old is over 48%. Mark was like one in five black men unemployed in Britain. At the time of his death, Mark was working to acquire a construction skills certification. "I would have done everything to help Mark with a job in construction," Shaun, a building services engineer, insisted.

When asked about the 1,400 folks who have died in police custody in the United Kingdom, Lord Judd declared, "We must completely change the culture of policing—police and community together". Frank, as he insisted on being called, was quick to note that all police where not bad. Lord Judd, a Labour Party member, served on the Joint Committee for Human Rights. The select committee issued "Deaths in Police Custody"study including testimony from family members of those who died by police shooting. "Several of the families had been informed of a death in ways that were highly insensitive, and several had been given insufficient information about what had happened, or had been obstructed in their attempts to obtain information" reads the 2004 report.

In the family's back yard—looking into the distance—Shaun echoed the Death in Police Custody report's findings, "Someone should have put our minds at rest." Laughing with a face full of tears, "Mark-a gangster, Ha!", Shaun shrugged. A now blank faced Shaun—starring into that same distance stated, "The police had a shoot to kill policy on my brother."   The family did not condone the riots that followed. "It takes away from what happened to Mark", Shaun feared.

Clouds hung over The Farm the morning of Mark's farewell—an ominous spirit hovering.   A crowd had begun to assemble on The Frontline. Gary closed the store for the day—greeted me. "You are cool. But these others guys cannot come over here" pointing to the other journalists—cordon off a block away from The Frontline. The guys that surrounded me during my first trip dapped me up. All fell silent as four white horses turned the corner. With white feathered head dressing, the stallions marched lock step carrying out the ancient cortège rite—a funeral procession through the deceased's community. Guided by two men in top hats and gray tuxedos with pinstripes and tails, white beauties drew a glass covered carriage with a bronze casket.

The carriage was garlanded with white and blue floral arrangements reading: Dad, Brother, and Son.   Trailed by eight stretch Mercedes Benz Limousines, the carriage stopped so that Mark and his mates hung out on The

Frontline. Community folks took pictures and video. Many of them came up and touched the glass. Most guys wore shades and tears dripped from their chins. Lex touched the carriage, tears rolled down his face, and he shook his head in disbelief.

Bishop Kwaku Frimpong-Mason, who commented that Mark was like a son, presided over the processional. Dressed in high ceremonial vestments—crowned with purple head covering, long purple robe, crimson stole, and a large silver cross—Bishop Kwaku urged onlookers to celebrate Mark's life. "Stretch for your hands" commanded the Bishop. The act of 'stretching forth hands' is a common gesture in Pentecostal faith communities—signifying god's blessing upon the one for whom the hands are directed.

The British media characterized the whole affair as a gangster send off. Reporting for ITV's London Tonight, Marcus Powell referred to the cortege as "a gangster tradition". The *Daily Mail* printed:

> His loved ones wanted to remember him as an innocent family man...But another side to Mark Duggan's life was evident too. It was there in the one-armed salute that men and women gave as the white, horse-drawn hearse passed along the streets from Duggan's family home in Tottenham

Escorted by a carriage attendant in top hat and tails, Shaun, Bruno, Bishop Kwaku, and his closest mates positioned themselves at the head of the regal mares—walking Mark's body out of The Farm for the last time.

The streets near Cathedral of Praise New Testament Church of God were teeming with people. Stafford and a Farm pastor wore white arm bands— keeping the church entrance clear. The old Dutch Reform church building built in 1909 with seating for about 1000. Well over 1500 people stood in the isles, sat on steps to the balcony, and the balcony itself was overflowing. Another thousand or so stood outside and listened to the service on outdoor speakers. A block away, herded behind metal fences, an international press corps constantly clicked their cameras mounted with telescopic lens.

On big flat screens, women lead the congregation in songs—extolling God's love and grace. The crowd stood as Shaun and Marlon helped to bring their brother to the altar. Aunt Carol, Pamela's sister, read Bruno and Pamela's tribute to their son. She lovingly recollected Mark's time with her in Manchester. "He got himself an education." Mark had begun the process to become a fireman. "He wanted to help his community," she told the flock. She, painfully, proclaimed: "He was my baby." Collecting herself, Aunt Carol declared, "Semone you are not just a rock. You are a wall."

And crowd exploded with applauds and cheers. Semone was too broken up to read her love letter to Mark. Her cousin, Donna Martin did the honors. "'Twisted' by Keith Sweat was our song. You were a family man and you loved your children and me," Donna read with one arm around a weeping Semone. Shaking with heartache, Semone was dressed like she was about to begin her life with Mark.

Dressed in a cream chiffon knee length dress and gold platform pumps—the straps accented with rhinestones— complimenting her perfect pitch black complexion. When

114

Kalyiah, their 18 months old, was not clinging to her mother, she ran about the pulpit causing pastors and family to give chase; bringing joy to the otherswise somber occasion.

Karen Hall, Mark's elder sister, tenderly read Tupac Shakur's poem "Fallen Star"—ending in lamentation: "What they have done for much 2 long/2 just forget and carry on/I had loved u forever because of who u r /And now I mourn our fallen star."

Donna opened the reading of obituary with "Starrish" prompting the congregation to applaud. The media carried the story that 'Starrish' was Mark gang name—pissing Lex off . "He was a kid who did the hip hop t'ing. Starrish him rapper name. He dressed well. Him like nice shiny t'ings, like bling. So dem young boys call him Starrish. Like a shining star, you know. Him no bad man, gun man gangsta." Lex told me several times.

"Starrish," Donna repeated to more applauds. Slowly and deliberately she recounted his life—interjecting antidotes—"Balance" was his favorite retort when someone was making much to do about something. When Donna got choked up and paused with emotion. "Balance" the crowd reminded her.

A subdued the Right Reverend Barrington Burrell read an under- whelming self empowerment sermon. Seldom looking up from his manuscript, Bishop Burrell urged the attentive gathering to seek a better life. "Stretch forth your hands", Rev. Nims Obunge charged the assembled.

Then the pastor of Freedom's Ark Church closed the service with a fervent prayer. The lanky cleric paced back and forth with long strides. A needful litany flowed like a mighty stream; "Bring that which is done in the dark to light", beseeched Nims— each supplication punctuated by "In the name of Jesus". Rev. Obunge lamented their collective lot, "We have been hurt!" "Amen" audience members responded. "We have been scarred! We have been maligned!"

"Yes we have." A young lady next to me testified.

Drawing deep rhythmic breaths, he whooped, "We have been stigmatized!" "We have been called names." Finality consumed Nim's tone, rebuking the media stereotypes, "Today, we stand as one community and say, 'Not any more – it shall stop.'"

As Mark's coffin returned to the carriage, Stafford and the other marshals directed the crowd to walk to cemetery. The immediate family gathered around the grave. Mark and Kelvin tombstones touch one another. Starrish and Smegz are buried head to head.

At least two thousand mourners silently observed the graveside service. Kemani, Kajuan, and Kalyiah released a single white dove setting off jubilation. White balloons ascended to heavens lifting everyone's spirits. Lowering the casket in the grave, "Ashes to Ashes, Dust to Dust," Bishop Kwaku committed Mark's remains to earth. It was finished.

But no one moved. Solemnly waiting as the cemetery staff placed the black steel cover over the grave. Unsure about how he died, they would be confident in his burial. Breaking into song, the burial ground became a sanctuary of hope.

Classic reggae tunes and traditional hymns saturated the late summer afternoon. The Farm serenaded Mark at his final resting place. Paraphrasing Bob Marley's Redemption Song, one mourner loudly pondered, "How long shall they kill our brothers while we stand aside and look?" Colin Sparrow, deputy senior investigator for the IPCC, estimated that the "complex investigation" into Duggan's death could take four to six months—too long

exiles in the promised land

I moved to New Orleans a year and half after the levees broke. I lived across the river from downtown in Algiers on the west bank of the Mississippi. Originally settled by Native Americans because the land rested on higher ground, Algiers did not flood but suffered extensive wind damage.

Each morning, around 7:30am, I would leave my four room shotgun house and walk to the neighborhood cafe, Tout de Suite, responding along the way to several patrons singing, "Good morning, Reverend." I would grab a stool at the coffee bar, drank a double cappuccino, and depart to a similar serenade, "Have a goodday, Reverend."

As I walked through the elegantly dressed streets of Old Algiers Point, I was amused by gawking small children in their strollers. Eventually, I would arrive at the west bank ferry dock, sitting down and smoking my pipe while gazing out at the muddy waters of the Mississippi. A few minutes later, boarding the ferry for the magical ride across the river, I would notice that my fellow ferry travelers were an eclectic mix of artists, anarchists, immigrants and exiles. I was struck most by those who wore maid and maintenance uniforms.

These men and women spoke with a unique musicality. Their term of endearment for one another—"baby"—was elongated and tuned in a minor key that would have made Louis Armstrong smile. But I cried. I cried everyday because their misery was tangible.

Upon arriving on the east bank, the ferry would dock at the edge of downtown, near the hotels and casinos. My fellow passengers were headed to what author Douglas Coupland called "McJobs"—low wage, low prestige, non-benefited work. In a city whose economy centers on tourism, there is only one union hotel. I would then board a street car to our offices. I had moved to New Orleans to serve as founding Executive Director of the Interfaith Worker Justice Center of New Orleans.

The unwritten part of my job description often called for me to conduct "devastation" tours for academics and activists who were visiting the city. They always requested to go to the ground zero of the greatest man made disaster in this nation's history-the Lower Ninth Ward.

While I was giving a tour of Lower Ninth Ward to a group of female sociologists visiting New Orleans for a race, class, and gender conference, a dialogue incurred that revealed more in what was not said than what was said. For miles, homes were torn from their foundations, democracy cracked to its core. One was overcome with a deep sense of sadness. Silence filled the air. Hope choked.

As our minivan crawled through the devastation, we would see the tour buses gawking at the misery of the poor of New Orleans. I would always point out to those with me that some of the houses were signed with an odd signature. It was not the infamous X with codes in each quadrant to signify the name of the unit that had searched the residence, its location, date of inspection, and the number of dead (humans and animals) inside. Instead, these houses simply read, "Baghdad." "Baghdad on the bayou," I thought, aloud.

One of my fellow tour guides, Abby Lublin, a New York City teacher who had spent a few months in New Orleans volunteering for the People's Organizing Committee, referred to human catastrophe in New Orleans as "genocide." The collection of distinguished academics and I engaged in a lively debate. We concluded that the word "genocide" pointed us in the right direction, but was insufficient to describe what had happened on August 29, 2005. (In fact, the use of the word genocide in reference to New Orleans may cheapen what is happening in Darfur.)

Once I saw a National Guard Humvee in the parking lot of a McDonald's. Moments later, several Guardsmen emerged—machine guns in hand—escorting two Black teenagers out in handcuffs. I later learned that National Guard personnel retain their weapons during their different deployments, and that most of the Guard troops in New Orleans had been redeployed from Iraq. As a result, the same guns that were used to "establish democracy" in Iraq were being used by members of the National Guard to secure the city of New Orleans. Unfortunately, this is not new.

Historically, black folk have had to contend with hegemonic forces denying them both the means to make ends meet and make meaning— in the country that purported itself to be the Promised Land—a city on the hill, the new Zion. I do not believe that there is a promised land – only exile. Intellectuals and human rights activists debated the use of the term "refuge" or "internally displaced person" to described the abandoned citizens. They were indeed, exiled in "The Promised Land."

The concept of exile is central because I believe that post-Katrina New Orleans and general hostility toward the poor in this nation – whose identity is built upon manifest destiny – has shown that America has no "home" for poor black folks. We find ourselves rolling a stone up the hill of democracy. It is a Camusian dialectic, perpetually hewing a stone of hope out of a mountain of despair; Martin Luther King Jr.'s theology encountering Sisyphus' tragedy.

While the genealogy of black folk in America is littered with examples of this absurdity— images of folks stranded on rooftops and packed in the New Orleans Superdome are newer -this tragedy, however, does maintain some uniqueness. New Orleans is a phenomenon. It is the birthplace of jazz—America's first original art form—and an extraordinary mix of cultures that is reflected in its food, architecture, skin tones, and social life. Jazz and gumbo embody democracy. Difference is sacred and makes use of individuality to produce a collective good. Yet it is also the potential death bed of democracy—her greatest disaster (both natural and human-made). Post-Katrina New Orleans is shaped by a historical set of issues and by a present-day "unholy trinity": mass familial displacement, mass fiscal divestment, and mass physical devastation. In a word, New Orleans is tragicomic.

Today, her plight has disappeared from much of the public memory. And, following a six-month tour in her bosom, I found that the struggle to rebuild the great city is tainted with an overriding burden of hopelessness and misunderstanding.

Osagyefo Uhuru Sekou

We are challenged to bring to bear an interdisciplinary analysis that affirms these historical realities—combining a nuanced vision of the present with an eye on a prophetic future. three books help point us in a direction of this kind of approach: *After the Storm: Black Intellectuals Explore the Meaning of Hurricane Katrina* (The New Press, 2006); *What Lies Beneath: Katrina, Race and the State of the Nation* (South End Press, 2007); and *There Is No Such Thing as a Natural Disaster: Race, Class, and Hurricane Katrina* (Routledge, 2006).

While each anthology approaches the post-Katrina America and race from a different vantage point, they all contend with the meaning of black suffering within American democracy.Before reading a word, each text calls up the angst of those tragic days in late August and September of 2005. All three covers bear gothic, Gordon Parks-style photographs — images that are nothing less than miserable grace their covers — immortalizing democracy's graphic elegy.

Those stark images lay the foundation for a series of sobering essays. The effects of the breached levees in 2005 are laid over a historical narrative of New Orleans, filled with endemic poverty and racism — to return New Orleans to its pre-Katrina state would be unjust. We are reminded in each text that fully one-quarter of African-American men and one-third of African-American women in New Orleans lived below the poverty line prior to Katrina.

As Bruce Katz detailed in "Concentrated Poverty in New Orleans and Other American Cities" (The Chronicle of Higher Education, 8/4/06):

On the very day the levees broke, the Census Bureau released a report on poverty in the nation, finding that Orleans Parish had a poverty rate of 23.2 percent, seventh highest among 290 large U.S. counties. Yet the economic hardships were shared unequally. Although African-American residents made up 67 percent of the city's total population, they made up 84 percent of its population below the poverty line. And those poor African-American households were highly concentrated in 47 neighborhoods of extreme poverty — that is, neighborhoods where the poverty rate topped 40 percent.

These realities coalesced in real-time as the nation watched thousands of fellow citizens left to their own devices in the face of a Category Five hurricane. My search for meaning during several months in the Lower Ninth Ward led me to demand, as have others:

Where was god? Why had not god intervened? It is a question of theodicy and democracy at once. How could a good god allow those whose existence was miserable before the storm be silent in such a moment of tragedy and need?

Two days after Katrina devastated the Gulf Coast, Columbia Christians for Life, a Religious Right anti-choice organization, put out a statement claiming that the satellite image of Hurricane Katrina looked like a six-week old fetus:

> The image of the hurricane ... with its eye already ashore at 12:32 p.m. Monday, August 29, looks like a fetus (unborn human baby) facing to the left (west) in the womb, in the early weeks of gestation (approx. 6 weeks). ... Even the orange color of the image is reminiscent of a commonly used pro-life picture of early prenatal development. ...

Louisiana has 10 child-murder-by-abortion centers. ... [F]ive are in New Orleans.

Preaching at Jerry Falwell's Liberty University, Rev. Franklin Graham predicted, "There's been satanic worship. There's been sexual perversion. God is going to use that storm to bring revival. God has a plan. God has a purpose." The connection between the war on terror and this god's favored hurricane was made by Chuck Colson, the former Watergate conspirator, now a conservative Christian leader:

> Katrina gave us a preview of what America would look like if we fail to fight the war on terror. "Did God have anything to do with Katrina?," people ask. My answer is, he allowed it and perhaps he allowed it to get our attention so that we don't delude ourselves into thinking that all we have to do is put things back the way they were and life will be normal again.

In his foreword to *After the Storm*, legal scholar Derrick Bell leaps to respond to my concern for god's absence. "How can we awaken that sense of humanity within us that some call God to address the needs of those whose plight is the fault of man, not God? Perhaps, as many theologians think, we should view God not as a superbeing somewhere up there who determines our fates and can, at will intervene in our lives."

After the Storm, effectively, contrasts these existential and theological questions with the human evidence of abandonment of responsibility. And black folks ain't exempt. In the book's introduction, Charles Ogletree highlights the Essence Festival, which annually attracts over 100,000 African Americans to the Superdome to R&B and neo-soul artists. It is a harsh juxtaposition with the image of masses stranded for days in that same structure. Similarly, John Valery White problematizes Mayor Ray Nagin's symbolic political leadership and questions his commitment to poor blacks.

Governmental neglect and malfeasance are, of course, at the heart of the discourse. David Troutt cites the history of urban ghettoization through public housing policy and construction in "Many Thousands Gone, Again." And writing from a hotel room in Canada, from which she watched the devastation unfold, Sheryl Cashin reconsiders the role of urban organizations in light of Kanye West's infamous proclamation, "George Bush doesn't care about black people."

Conversely, Adolph Reed lambastes the focus on race. In his terse essay, "The Real Divide," Reed incisively highlights the role of class. He rejects race as the primary tool of analysis for two reasons: first, "the language of race and racism is too imprecise to describe effectively even how patterns of injustice and inequality are racialized in a post-Jim Crow world." Second, Reed argues that many liberals gravitate to the language of racism not simply because it makes them feel righteous but also because is doesn't carry any political warrant beyond exhorting people not to be racist. Reed contends that use of race obscures class and does not recognize a fundamental crisis in the political economy.

Racism, for Reed, "can be a one-word description and explanation of patterns of unequal distribution of income and wealth, services and opportunities, police brutality, a stockbrokers inability to get a cab, neighborhood dislocation and gentrification, poverty, unfair criticism of black or Latino athletes, or being denied admission to a boutique. Because the category is so porous, it doesn't explain anything. Indeed, it is to an alternative explanation."

Yet race must be addressed as we consider the phenomenon of New Orleans. Focusing on the descriptions of a black man carrying a bag as a "looter" and a white couple as having "found" food, Cheryl I. Harris and Devon W. Carbado investigate the role of racial logic in articulating the activities of stranded residents in the flood's immediate aftermath. "Loot or Find? Fact or Frame" strives to unmask the color-blind discourse surrounding race in the American media. Michael Eric Dyson skilfully categorizes the forms of migration experienced by black folk and situates Katrina in that context. Clement Alexander Price methodologically discusses the Galveston, Texas flood of 1900, finding poor blacks to be peculiarly vulnerable to nature disasters.

These essays and others counter Reed's claim of race being inappropriate to describe this current crisis. His claim obscures the blackness of suffering in late modernity. Where Reed is correct is in saying that race and class need to engage in a more intimate dialogue — and within that conversation we also need to include gender.

In *There Is No Such Thing as a Natural Disaster*, that linkage is made most evident in an essay by co-editor Chester Hartman and social policy analyst Avis Jones-DeWeever. In "Abandoned Before the Storms," the coauthors illustrate with wonkish precision the dismal unemployment and poverty rates for African-American women. "In fact, of the 43 states with sample sizes large enough to provide a reliable measure of African-American women's earnings, Louisiana ranked worst in the nation with full-time annual earnings of only $19,400."

Margaret Morganroth Gullette's chapter, "Katrina and the Politics of Later Life," provide a unique argument. "Ageism," she theorizes, "at the level of feelings is a peculiar privilege, compelling but ominous." Ageism has this in common with racism or sexism: it forbids thinking "we can ever be them."

People over 50 died in far greater numbers in the storm's aftermath. These unwarranted deaths are linked to an ideology of decline, writes Gulette. "Ageism is wrapped up in neo-liberal state policy on behalf of post-industrial capital. Power, not the needs of the woman on the baggage mover or the 45-year-old on workers' comp, drives the ideology of declines." Our national state, like others, is "promoting and funding market solutions" in a "race to the bottom" to see "how much and how fast social expenditures may be reduced in order to transfer more national wealth to the corporate sector." This is a global effort, she maintains. The World Bank and the International Monetary Fund are "at the forefront of attempts to foster a political climate conducive to reducing the state welfare of old age."

The insertions of ageism and gender to the Katrina discourse speak to the level of nuance needed to understand what has been unmasked about American "democracy" — and the global economy. Filled with graphs and numbers, *There Is No Such Thing* provides insights on the role of financial institutions alongside grassroots organizing, medical needs, pre and post-public education crisis and the public housing. The book's most important element is that it puts forth a strong set of policies — ones that would not rebuild New Orleans, but create a deeper democracy.

What Lies Beneath offers a chorus of indigenous voices. Like a jazz band, steeped in improvisation, the work is the most heartfelt and wise of the three. Edited by the South End Press collective, the book is both dramatic and elegant.

The personal struggles for survival are absent from the other pair of anthologies. This collection poignantly retells several of these stories. Charmine Neville, of the famous musical family, painfully recounts being raped. She then describes how, despite such a violation, she continued — like Harriet Tubman — to go back and get those who had been left behind. In her simply titled essay, "How We Survived the Flood," she recalls:

There was a group of us, there were about 24 of us, and we kept going back and forth and rescuing whoever we could get and bringing them to the French Quarter because we heard there were phones in the French Quarter, and that there wasn't any water. And they were right, there were phones but we couldn't get through to anyone. I found some police officers. I told them that a lot of us women had been raped down there by guys, not from the neighborhood where we were, they were helping us to save people.

The question of violence during Katrina and its aftermath is a problematic, layered one. In "To Render Ourselves Visible," the radical feminist collective INCITE! Women of Color Against Violence editors problematize the topic by looking both at how some survivors were criminalized as well as the silence by organizers and analysts on the question of sexual violence against women and children. This leads them to declare:

Instead of figuring out strategies to take people's experiences of sexual violence seriously, the strategy was to bring the media's attention back to the "real" problems of institutional poverty, police violence, and the failure of government response. Sexual violence (along with its victims and perpetrators) is, again, rendered invisible in the name of ending racism.

With a broad lens of critique, the INCITE! authors also point to how outside organizations and individuals ignored local leadership — and how women of color from New Orleans have organized themselves in response. Throughout the anthology, women's and other voices from New Orleans are lifted up; not as a footnote, but rather a powerful testimony to the endurance of the poor, and those who are their chosen representatives. The stories of community groups — like Common Ground, the People's Hurricane Relief Fund, and the Black Women's Health Project — are told by the organizers themselves.

What Lies Beneath also succeeds by evoking the tales of suffering through different forms of writing. The poetic pen of Kalamu ya Salaam and Suheir Hammad lend beauty to the pain of this experience. Jared Sexton's stirring essay, "The Obscurity of Black Suffering," illustrates the invisibility of poor black folk both inside and outside of the black community. Sexton's notion of obscurity sits at the center of my own sense of emptiness concerning New Orleans where I cried every day for six months.

While the Interfaith Worker Justice Center that I went to New Orleans is up and running, staffed with interns, I still felt defeated. Perhaps, it is because New Orleans taught me what I did not know. My faith was shaken; my vocation questioned; my sense of professional success shattered; and any messianic impulse that I have ever possessed receded with the floodwaters. I have gained a deeper appreciation of the work of everyday folk to change their lot. Like faith itself, the local organizers of New Orleans are the substance of what I hoped for and the evidence of what I could not see.

about the author

Rev. Osagyefo Uhuru Sekou authored the critically acclaimed *urbansouls* and is an ordained Elder in the Church of God in Christ (Pentecostal). He has held fellowships at the Brooklyn Society for Ethical Culture, The Fellowship of Reconciliation, Catholics for a Free Choice, and New York Theological Seminary's Micah Institute. He has given over 1000 lectures throughout the country and abroad, including Harvard Divinity School, Princeton University, University of Virginia, the University of Paris IV-La Sorbonne, Ta-Maturuk Library (Beirut, Lebanon), World Culture Center (Berlin, Germany), and Bahcesehir University (Istanbul, Turkey).

Rev. Sekou produced and directed the short documentary film, *Exiles in the Promised Land: The Quest for Home*. Recognizing his distinguished work as public intellectual, the Institute for Policy Studies-appointed Rev. Sekou as an Associate Fellow in Religion and Justice. Rev. Sekou received the Keeper of the Flame Award 2011 by the National Voting Rights Institute and Museum in Selma, AL.

For more information visit: **www.revsekou.org**

Made in the USA
Lexington, KY
19 April 2012